Preparing the Portfolio

for an Assessment of Prior Learning

Revised Edition

Revised Edition
Copyright ©1980, 1999, 2001 Roslyn Snow
Printed in the United States of America

All rights reserved. No part of this book may be reproduced or transmitted in any form or by any means, electronic or mechanical, including photocopying, recording or by any information storage and retrieval system, without permission in writing from the author.

ISBN: 1-4196-7384-X
ISBN-13: 978-1419673849

Visit www.booksurge.com to order additional copies.

PREPARING THE PORTFOLIO

for an Assessment of Prior Learning

Revised Edition

Roslyn Snow

Contents

Suggested Schedule for Completing the APL Program   vi

Chapter One: The APL Program   **1**
Preliminary Exercise: Analyzing a Task   5

Chapter Two: Writing the Essay   **7**
Exercise 1: The Chronology   7
Exercise 2: Writing About Your Work Experience   11
Exercise 3: Education and Training; Life Experience   29
Exercise 4: The Introduction   34

Chapter Three: Documenting the Essay   **37**
Exercise 5: Writing Solicitation Letters   37
Exercise 6: Documents and Document Signals   43

Exercise 7: Index to Documents   54

Chapter Four: Choosing Transferable Credits   **61**
Exercise 8: Request for Credit   64

Chapter Five: Petitioning for Credit   **79**
Exercise 9: Writing the Petition   80

Chapter Six: Assembling the Portfolio   **85**
Exercise 10: Front Matter   86
Exercise 11: Assembling the Portfolio   90

Chapter Seven: Assessment   **99**
Exercise 12: Revision, Final Submission   99

Copyright ©1980, 1999, 2001 Roslyn Snow

Suggested Schedule for Completing the APL Program

Chapter 1   The APL Program   1 week
...What is APL? APL stands for Assessment of Prior Learning – a program to allow you to convert the knowledge gained from your work experience to accredited, transferable college credits. You get a "jump-start" toward your bachelor's degree!

Chapter 2   Writing the Essay   10 weeks
...The APL essay is a long one. It is about every job you had from the time you first started work. Your instructor will help you every step of the way and day by day. You write a series of essays, one at a time, and wait for instructor critique before going on. Our way of helping you write your essay will assure that you receive the maximum course credits you deserve.

Chapter 3   Documenting the Essay   3 weeks
...Better than a resume, you will prepare a career album of all your accomplishments at work to showcase your APL essay.

Chapter 4   The Catalog Search   1 week
...Your instructor will help you find the courses to request for college credit. These will be courses you need for your bachelor's degree.

Chapter 5   Petition for Credit   3 weeks
...We show you how to match the knowledge you have to the college courses you request.

Chapter 6   Assembling the Portfolio 3 weeks
...You will put together your essays, your showcase documents and your petitions into an album – a career album – to gain college credits and future career advancement.

Chapter 7   Assessment   3 weeks
...Your instructor will take charge of your portfolio now. Qualified college faculty members who will award your college credits will read it. Your results will be placed on your official college transcript, which will be sent to the college or university of your choice. You will know what courses to take to complete your college degree.

Copyright ©1980, 1999, 2001 Roslyn Snow

Chapter One: The APL Program

Over the past years, I have had the privilege of guiding adults through the process of an assessment of their prior learning. This text is the result of their labors through my guidance. Each adult received academic credits from an accredited college for learning acquired in life, at home and on-the-job.

You can look forward to preparing a career album or portfolio that will earn college credits. Get ready for the thrill of a lifetime: looking back at all you have learned and ahead to your march down the aisle to receive your college degree.

--Roslyn Snow

WELCOME TO APL

THE APL PROGRAM

APL, or Assessment of Prior Learning, is a program in which an accredited college assesses learning you received prior to coming to their campus. You acquired this learning through experience. It will be the task of the college to measure or assess the learning that resulted. We will teach you how to prove your learning and experience is college level. The college will award credits for your work and life experience toward a degree.

ARE YOU QUALIFIED FOR APL?

Nothing is more frustrating than entering a program with high hopes of reaching a goal only to hit a snag mid-way through. If only you could have anticipated what was to happen. Full disclosure of the demands of the program could have alerted you right at the start.

To discover how suited you are to this program, complete the following questionnaire by checking each statement that applies to you.

Copyright ©1980, 1999, 2001 Roslyn Snow

☐ I have worked at one job for at least five years since entering the job market.

☐ Over the years of working at a job or various jobs I have advanced from routine work to work requiring more skill and responsibility over others.

☐ I have taken training seminars or workshops offered by my employer, union or other source, or taken adult education courses in the community or through private schools.

☐ I have the commitment and the time (over six hours a week) necessary to devote to this program, and I have an educational goal to receive a bachelor's degree.

☐ I have the writing skill to compose an essay without serious errors in grammar and spelling. I can correct my writing errors with minimal help.

Each statement sets minimal guidelines for the APL program.

☑ You must have had a stable work background, doing work that advanced in difficulty and in responsibility over time.

☑ To keep up in your field you had to receive advanced training. Now you have chosen an educational goal: a college degree. APL will help you receive credits to move you toward your goal without repeating courses in areas you already know and use at work.

☑ You must have time to devote to this program. You will need to write a long essay – perhaps as long as 30 to 50 pages. You will have to assemble documents to verify your experiences. You will need to assemble a Portfolio following a special format.

☑ You must be able to write sentences and paragraphs free of major errors and be able to correct your own errors with minimal help.

Copyright ©1980, 1999, 2001 Roslyn Snow

EXPERIENCE ALONE IS NOT LEARNING

Many educators realize that learning occurs outside the classroom and that self-starters are able to reach the same level of skills and knowledge as those whose learning was designed by a teacher in a college classroom.

APL program developers recognize, however, that experience alone is not always a competent teacher. Other ingredients are necessary. The experience must be repeated often enough to allow for improvement. The learner must have improvement of ability as a goal. He or she must be modeling the repetitions according to a standard conceived or observed. He has seen that experience done better or he has an image of improvement in his mind. The learner must see experiences in relation to each other. He must be able to break them down into parts and sequences. The learner ought to be able to think about and communicate what learning occurred.

Infrequent exposure to an experience will not result in much learning. On the other hand, tedious repetition of experience will result in learning only if there is some thinking involved—thinking about learning itself: getting better, seeing relationships, remembering what was experienced and communicating it.

If this were not true, your APL Instructor could have you prepare a resume of your jobs, training, hobbies, and life experiences and submit this list to the college for credits. But the college is not as interested in the jobs you held and the experiences you had as in the outcomes of these experiences: what improvement you made, what relationships you drew, and most important, your ability to look back over your experience, remember it, and communicate it.

Copyright ©1980, 1999, 2001 Roslyn Snow

PREPARING THE PRELIMINARY EXERCISE

In the Preliminary Exercise, you will learn to think about your experience in a new way. Just as a teacher designs experiences for students to learn from, you will look at an experience you have had in terms of what it has taught you. This exercise will not be a part of your Portfolio. Only your APL Instructor will see it.

Think about a routine task you performed at home within the last few days: sewing a button on a shirt; removing a stain; building a bookcase; changing the oil in your car; fixing a meal. List the steps you took to get the task done. Then list what you learned from this task or what you would have been expected to know in order to do it.

EXAMPLE
TASK: ASSEMBLING A BOOKCASE
STEPS:
1. Measure space
2. List and buy materials
3. Cut wood pieces for sides
4. Cut board for back
5. Cut grooves in side panels
6. Assemble and glue
7. Add braces and screws
8. Attach to wall studs
9. Paint

WHAT I LEARNED:
1. How to use light tools, measuring tape, level, drill, saw, hammer
2. How to estimate board feet
3. How to choose wood
4. How to apply glue and clamp
5. How to locate stud in wall
6.. How to mix paint, use roller and paint brush

Copyright ©1980, 1999, 2001 Roslyn Snow

Preliminary Exercise: Analyzing a Task

YOUR TURN: Choose a simple task and break it into steps. Then list what you needed to know in order to perform the task.

TASK: (Choose a simple task you do at home. Do not choose a task you perform at work.)

STEPS:

1.
2.
3.
4.
5.
6.
7.
8.

WHAT I LEARNED:
1.
2.
3.
4.
5.

> Send your Preliminary Exercise to your instructor by e-mail or fax as soon as possible. This exercise needs to be approved before you can go on.

Copyright ©1980, 1999, 2001 Roslyn Snow

Chapter Two: Writing the Portfolio Essays

Exercise 1: THE CHRONOLOGY

Outline the sections your essay will contain. The **Chronology** will be the working outline for your portfolio essay. The three sections of your essay will be:

1. Work Experience
2. Education and Training
3. Life Experience.

Complete The Worksheets

The worksheets on the following pages will help you gather the facts you need for your outline or Chronology. <u>**Save this information on your computer hard drive and on storage disc.**</u>

Your Work Experience

List the jobs you have held since you were 18 years old, including the rank and position you held in the military. Include the name of the company, the city and state, the dates you were employed, the position and the duties you performed. Start with your earliest job. *List each position you held as a separate job.* Use your own paper to complete these tables. Save your work on your computer hard drive or disc.

Dates	Employer	City/State	Position	Duties

Copyright ©1980, 1999, 2001 Roslyn Snow

Education and Training

List all training you received on-the-job, at vocational or proprietary schools or in community programs. Do not list courses for which you received accredited course credit. Save your work on your computer hard drive or disc.

Dates	Name of Course	Sponsor	Topics Covered	Hours

Life Experience

List hobbies, sports, civic activities, and volunteer or community experiences. List self-employment. Include memberships in community organizations or service clubs. List private instruction in music, art, flying. List personal improvement programs. Save your work on your computer hard drive or disc.

Dates	Activity	Organization

Copyright ©1980, 1999, 2001 Roslyn Snow

Use the information you have listed on the three worksheets to prepare your Chronology.

Title the page **Chronology**

Add these subtitles:

Subtitle	**Work Experience**
List all the information on your Work Experience worksheet.

Subtitle	**Education and Training**
List all the information on your Training worksheet.

Subtitle	**Life Experience**
List all the information on your Life Experience worksheet.

All lists should be in chronological order starting with your *earliest* job or activity. Most students begin their work experience with the job they had at age 18. Each section will contain its facts in chronological order.

Send your **Chronology** to your Instructor now. Wait for your Instructor's critique before going on to the next assignment.

Copyright ©1980, 1999, 2001 Roslyn Snow

More About... Your Chronology

Your Instructor has reviewed your previous assignment and told you of any needed changes or revisions.

■ Often students will start their Chronology with their current job, as they would on a resume. It is better to start with your earliest job. Your Portfolio essays will reflect your job changes and mobility from early jobs up through your current, more complex career position. You may have been asked to make this change to your Chronology.

■ You may not have listed each position you held with the company or organization. It is better to break down each job into different positions so that you can show the added responsibilities you had and the promotions you received. You may have been asked to make this change to your Chronology.

Exercise 2: WRITING ABOUT YOUR WORK EXPERIENCE

Begin with the first job listed in your Chronology. Eventually you will write about each job you held using the simple format that follows. For now, write only about your FIRST job. The format that follows will help you get started if you are having trouble beginning this assignment. **Use it if you need to. As you progress you may abandon this format for your own personal style.** Save all of your work on your computer hard drive or disc.

Use a Heading for Each Separate Essay

Begin each essay segment with a HEADING as follows.

NAME OF COMPANY (or ORGANIZATION)
CITY, STATE
DATES EMPLOYED
JOB TITLE Each new job title or position will be a separate essay, even if you remained at the same company or organization. Therefore, you will need to insert a new heading before each new essay.

Introduce the Company You Worked For

I worked for_____ as a _____
_____ from_____(date)_
_____to_____. This company (or department) specialized in _____
_____.

Tell Where You Worked and What You Did

I worked in the department that handled_____.
My major duty was to _____.

Copyright ©1980, 1999, 2001 Roslyn Snow

To complete this duty, I did several tasks. For instance, I would _____
_____
_____
_____.

Tell How You Performed Each Duty

Each of these tasks required smaller steps to accomplish.

First, I would _____.

Then I would_____.

My last step would be to _____.

Continue to Write About Each of Your Duties

I was also responsible for _____.

In order to complete this duty, I followed a set procedure. First I _____
_____.

Then I _____. Last, I _____
_____.

Tell If You Left For a New Job or a Promotion

I left this job because_____.

Copyright ©1980, 1999, 2001 Roslyn Snow

You Are Beginning a Long Range Project: The Portfolio Essay

Each job that you write about will be a separate **essay**. When you have written about all of your jobs, you will compile these essays into one large **Portfolio Essay** that covers all of your jobs. You may have many job positions if you remained at one company for a long time. Every new job position will be a new essay. Every time you changed companies, you will be writing about a different job assignment.

Your Portfolio Essay will be a compilation of all of these smaller essays. You will write one essay at a time. **Wait for feedback and suggestions from your Instructor before moving to the next essay.**

Let your Instructor help you find problems in your writing while there is time to correct them, before you make the same error in another essay.

Including Detail in Your Essay

It is important to include as much detail as you can in your essay, even in an essay about a job you held 15 to 20 years ago!

Here are some hints for including sufficient detail in your Essay:

- ✓ If you are responsible for a process, give it a name.
    "I'm responsible for inspecting suture rings."
- ✓ Tell what is involved.
    "I'm lead inspector over ten inspectors who check 500 suture rings daily for flaws in welding, assembly and polishing."
- ✓ Break your job duty into tasks and equipment or procedures
    "I flow-test, leak test and perform microscopic visual inspection at 20X."
- ✓ Visualize yourself working on an average day. Write the steps you take any given hour to finish a job.
- ✓ Think of yourself about to go on a holiday. Write the list of steps your replacement needs to do your job correctly.

Copyright ©1980, 1999, 2001 Roslyn Snow

- ✓ Get a work sample (a schematic, a report, a set of procedures you wrote, a form you created). Explain how you did it and what it means.

- ✓ Write in "active voice," using the personal pronoun "I" in most of your sentences:
    <u>I</u> buffed the gears.
    <u>I</u> composed letters to customers.
    <u>I</u> installed circuits.
    <u>I</u> keyed data at a speed of 120 wpm.
    <u>I</u> developed cost analyses and presented them in writing to my supervisor.

- ✓ Use identifying brand names of equipment or procedures.
    ```
    I prepared reports and correspondence using
    Microsoft Word. I used Microsoft PowerPoint to
    create visuals for my supervisor's briefings. I
    used Microsoft Publisher to prepare flyers and
    order forms.
    ```

More detail is better than less. **Try to remember as many details as you can.**

Your first essay will not be as detailed, as long, or as complex as later essays. Your first job required few skills and involved much repetition. Whatever was required of you in this position, be as clear and as thorough as you can in writing about it.

Two questions will be in your reader's mind as your essay is being evaluated:

1. *How* did you perform the tasks?
2. *Why* did you choose one course of action or one way of doing things over another?

Have these questions in mind as you describe your working day. If, for example, you chose an open letter format in typing or formatting a business letter, or decided to right-justify your work, have an explanation for your choice. If your choice was governed by an existing office or shop procedure, explain that.

If you made the decision as a machinist to replace a machine tool tell why. In doing so you will show your knowledge of the procedures you followed.

As you write your essay, remember that the evaluators will determine what you *learned* by reading what you *show* them. *You do not have to state what you learned.* Leave that to the evaluators to decide. You need to tell the evaluators what you did at each job, how, and why.

> Send your Instructor your first essay now. Your APL Instructor will review your essay before you go on the next job listed in your chronology. If your Instructor is confident that you are on the right track and have included enough detail about your work experience, you can go on writing about the next job or position in this same way. Wait for your Instructor's response to each essay before continuing.

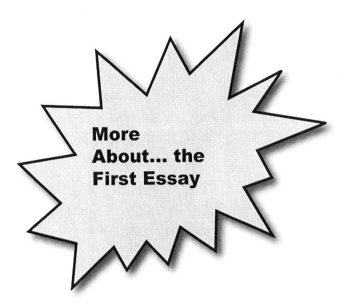

Early Essay Problems

> Your Instructor has reviewed your first essay. If it was well written, your Instructor has told you to go on to the next position, following your Chronology. Or you may need more help. Two problems often mar the first few essays in the Portfolio: stilted writing style and not enough detail.

Correcting a Stilted Writing Style

Your Instructor may have told you that your first essay was written in a mechanical fashion. This problem can be remedied. You may have excellent detail in this essay, but you have followed the organizational format in this chapter too closely so that your essay appears stilted or mechanical.

The organizational format gives you a place to start. It is like the basting on a hem. You want it there until you have put in all your beautiful stitches so that the hem does not become uneven or puckered. Once all your final stitches are in, you can remove the basting. Similarly, when you have completed your essay segment, you can edit and refine your style before you submit your assignment.

Copyright ©1980, 1999, 2001 Roslyn Snow

Try for a more conversational style in your essay by varying the way you start each paragraph rather than repeating "another duty" or "my next duty" so frequently. You can use transitions such as "*While* I monitored the switchboard, I *also* typed short memos and filed invoices."

Refine your first essay, giving it more of a personal or conversational style and send your revision to your APL Instructor.

Adding Detail to Your Essay

Your essay may be written in a lovely style, thoroughly relaxed and conversational. Yet, it may contain too little detail. You may say simply that you wrote letters for your employer and ran the office while the manager was out. You may say that you made travel arrangements for the department. You may say that you prepared drawings from engineer's notes. Your APL Instructor has returned your essay for revision to include *how* you completed each of these duties.

You should write specific explanations of *how* you drafted and finalized the correspondence for your employer, step by step, including how you got the information, how you outlined the letter, whether you used a typewriter or computer keyboard, what format you used, how you proofread and how you backed up and filed the letter, memo, or report. You need to tell what kind of vocabulary you used and whether you needed to use special features like tabbed columns, captions, insertions or merged text. You need to quantify this task, telling how often you wrote letters, how long they were, and how many you might write in a given period.

Copyright ©1980, 1999, 2001 Roslyn Snow

In the same way, you can detail how you made travel arrangements. What forms did you use for authorization? Did you use a travel agent? Did you prepare a purchase order? Did you keep a file or a computer database for budgeting? Did you process reimbursement?

Similarly, you would detail how you prepared a drawing. You would include information about the engineering notes. Tell what kinds of information were included. What was the purpose of the drawing? Then tell how you began the drawing, how you included all the items on the engineers' notes, and what drafting tools you used and how you used them. Describe the finished drawing: its format, size, content, symbols, and accompanying notes or lists.

Perhaps your essay did not cover correspondence, travel arrangements, or drawings. Perhaps your essay was about filling orders at Sandwich Shop or bagging groceries at the local chain store. You can apply the lessons learned on these pages to your specific job story, adding the detail that will make the experience come alive for the reader and convince the evaluator that you were there, doing these job tasks in exactly the way you describe them. The details you will include in your essay will be different from another student's details, and they will be different from the examples included in this text.

Send your revision, adding plenty of detail to it from your own work experience. Submit it, confident of a better reception.

CONTINUING THE ESSAY

As your Instructor guides you, complete a separate essay for each section of your work experience. Each position you held, even if in the same company, should be a separate story. Use a separate heading for each essay you write. Even if your next essay is about a different position at the same company, repeat the heading. Add the new dates for the new position and add the new job title. Send your essays to your Instructor in a regular, timely way. Wait for a specific critique on each essay before sending the next.

Copyright ©1980, 1999, 2001 Roslyn Snow

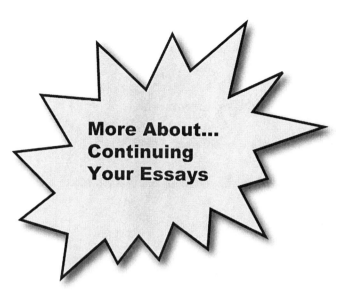

Making Progress Completing Your Essays

> Your Instructor has reviewed your previous assignment. If your essay was written well, your Instructor has told you to go on to the next position listed on your Chronology. If you needed to make any changes or revisions, your Instructor has told you. You may have had a problem in one of these areas:
> - Finding your uniqueness
> - Identifying your job duties
> - Orienting the reader
> - Writing in active voice
>
> Your Instructor will want you to read the following tips.

Find Your Uniqueness

Your APL Instructor has found that you repeated many of the job duties and tasks that you wrote in your previous essay. You are wondering what to do to correct this problem because you told the truth: You did the same tasks in both jobs. In fact, you may have had several different jobs in which you had the same responsibilities. You may have been a billing clerk at three different companies. You may have been a stocker at three different food markets. You machined parts at three different machine shops. What should you do?

Copyright ©1980, 1999, 2001 Roslyn Snow

They way you performed each job has your unique fingerprint. Each job you did is different. Search for these differences.

- Perhaps you used different equipment to do the same job.

- Perhaps the procedures you followed were different.

- Were there more customers included in the database you maintained?

- Were the customers different in any way?

- Is there one remembered story that stands out in one of these job experiences that you can re-tell as an example of how you did your work?

- Was there one customer you helped in a special way?

- Was there one report whose deadline you met despite difficult obstacles?

You can write, "My job duties remained the same, except…" and then explain the parts of the job that were different. Perhaps you used different equipment or helped to convert from old to new equipment. Perhaps your department was now larger and you served more customers or interfaced with more agencies. Perhaps there are one or two examples or memories you can re-tell that will illuminate the novel features of the jobs.

> Submit your revised essay, replacing the repeated material with fresh remembrances of those tools, procedures, customers or novel and unique examples.

Identifying Your Job Duties

- Your Instructor is not sure what your job responsibilities were. **Be sure to list your job duties.**

- Your Instructor does not know what tasks you did. **List and take us step by step through each task.**

Copyright ©1980, 1999, 2001 Roslyn Snow

- Your Instructor does not know what tools you used or what systems or procedures you followed. Each time you mention a task that involved a tool, system, procedure or reference aid, identify it (preferably by brand name).

Orienting the Reader

Your Instructor may be unsatisfied with your essay for another reason. You may be writing new material in each essay, but it is difficult for the reader to *picture* you on the job. **Set the scene.**

- Describe the building in which you worked. Describe the office or cluster of offices in which you worked or the shop floor on which you worked.

- Tell what your company or organization did or does. What is the product you were making or the outcome of your task?

- Describe the other workers and tell more about the workflow. Where did your work come from? Who received it from you? Did you meet with worker colleagues to complete projects or to discuss your work assignments? Did you interact with customers or the public? Did you travel to other sites to do your business?

- Describe the equipment in your work environment. If you had a printer queue, where was the printer? Did you travel to a mailroom or a file room? Was there a metrology room or workrooms that were specially designed for a procedure? Did you escort patients and prepare them for examinations in different rooms or cubicles? Help the reader picture your work environment in each of your jobs. Make the reader feel at home.

Then, "walk through" a typical day on the job. Start early in your daily routine when your shift begins. Take us step by step through your typical routine. If you do not have a typical routine, then "walk through" a day you remember on the job and tell what you did.

Copyright ©1980, 1999, 2001 Roslyn Snow

Write in Active Voice

Your Instructor is not sure what you did because you wrote in the passive voice. Instead of writing, "**I submitted** the report to the Board of Trustees," you wrote, "The report was submitted." No one knows who submitted it. **Use active verbs and "I" statements throughout your essays.** You establish your credibility and accountability by writing in first person and claiming that you actively performed the duties and tasks you have described.

What Is Your Purpose in Writing Your Essays?

At this point it will help you to know your purpose in using so much detail in your essays. Who will read your essays and what are they looking for?

In another few months, a team of faculty members from an accredited college will be reading and evaluating your completed Portfolio. Each faculty member will have training in different academic and vocational areas. Only one faculty member will have training in your area of job expertise.

For instance, if you are an administrative assistant, only one faculty member will evaluate office and computer information services courses. That faculty member will understand your job and may appreciate how well you explain it. Two other faculty members may not know about the programs or procedures you use. These faculty members will need to have very clear explanations. Your essays have to be so detailed that each faculty member can follow your explanations and your description of *how* you do your job.

In that same team meeting, one faculty member is curious to know how he or she can be sure you actually wrote your essay. Could you have copied your essay from company materials? Could you have read a book about the procedures you describe and simply summarized the book?

This is a concern in a distance-learning program in which the teachers may never meet the student in person. You need to use such good detail, such unique examples, and such thorough "walk throughs" that the faculty member has no doubt that you wrote from your own experience and knowledge.

Copyright ©1980, 1999, 2001 Roslyn Snow

You must write in active voice, using the personal pronoun "I" to signify that you performed the duties and tasks and experienced the learning you are describing.

✓ **The detail you add to your essays makes it easier to earn the *maximum course credits*. If the college granting the course credits also assigns grades, it is to your advantage to work hard in writing your essays so that you will merit the highest possible grades.**

Send each revision or new essay to your APL Instructor. Be sure your essay describes your job duties, orients the reader by setting the scene, uses vivid detail and active voice.

Guidelines As You Continue to Write Your Essays

MANAGEMENT RESPONSIBILITIES

As you move forward chronologically in your work experience, you may write about your management of work projects and your supervision of employees. These guidelines will help as you write about these job duties:

✓ How many workers do you supervise?
✓ Do you assign work?
✓ Do you evaluate job performance?
✓ Do you hire and fire personnel?
✓ How do you handle employee motivation?
✓ How do you handle poor work, absenteeism, and discipline?

Copyright ©1980, 1999, 2001 Roslyn Snow

✓ Do you interview candidates for employment?

✓ Walk through a typical day at work.

Write about each guideline that applies to your job. Tell HOW you performed each of these supervisory duties. Give examples. If you remember stories about employees you supervised, tell them. Choose stories or anecdotes that show your problem solving abilities and your skill working with difficult people or people in difficult situations.

When you "walk through" a typical day at your office or work site, start with your arrival at work. Tell the various tasks you have to perform to plan for your day, whether signing in, checking equipment, going over your calendar or schedule. Give examples of tasks you perform at certain times or stages of your workday. Tell who you contact, what meetings you attend, what paperwork or shop work you perform. If you are on a field site, describe your travel.

The "walk through" is a way to bring the faculty evaluators who will be reading your Portfolio Essay along with you to work. Just as these faculty members would be watching you perform hands-on assignments in a classroom, they want to be able to see you perform many of these same tasks on the job. You can help them visualize you in these work settings by describing what you are doing.

For instance, if you were in a word processing classroom your instructor would be able to look over your shoulder and watch as you set margins, created macros, chose design elements or set page layout on a document you created. You can write about these steps and procedures in such a way that the faculty evaluator can visualize your performance just from reading your essay.

A marketing instructor would be able to watch you work with a small group of students in class on a marketing plan for a small company as a school project. He could listen to your group discuss ideas. He could watch you sketch flyers, write ads, and make media buy selections. Help the marketing faculty evaluator by describing how you created a real marketing plan, or elements of such a plan, as part of a work assignment. List some of the ideas you came up with and the reasons for them. Tell how you made your selection of media and tell how you created the ads, how you chose color, how you chose text forms, how you decided what to highlight and how you chose words in the text. Describe the meetings you attended and those you chaired. Tell what was discussed and what was decided at these meetings. Give the marketing instructor a similar basis for evaluating you as though you were in his class.

A typical "walk through" might cover three or four separate pages in your essay segment. *More is better.*

Decision-Making on the Job

The jobs you are writing about may involve higher levels of responsibility in supervision or management of projects. At these levels, it is not enough to list and describe job duties. You may be starting to make decisions on the job: which customer to finance, which vendor to use, which employee to hire or promote or terminate? You will need to tell HOW you made these decisions.

Writing a Case History

A good way to do this is by writing a case history or extended example. Write about the hiring of an employee as a project you accomplished. Tell the history, how the position became available. Take us step by step through the process of selecting a candidate, interviewing, asking the right questions, listening for certain responses, reading body language, evaluating references and other documentation, following the proper human resources regulations. The reader is looking for your fingerprint in each of these case histories or examples, your unique way of handling issues on the job.

Perhaps the decision involves a new computer information system. Tell the history. How was the money for this purchase justified? What were the objectives of the purchase? How did you secure bids? How did you examine each vendor's presentation? How did you bring together users and managers to exchange information? How did you reach consensus?

Your essay may have been about how you put together a major presentation using PowerPoint or another presentation graphics program for the directors meeting. Walk us step by step through the process. Add the details as you lived them. Tell how you prepared the storyboards for the project and drafted the script. Tell the different computer commands and functions you needed to know to operate the software and design the visuals.

Copyright ©1980, 1999, 2001 Roslyn Snow

Cross-over Skills

Your ability to analyze difficult projects will be instrumental in your earning a variety of college credits through your assessment. If you are writing about your job as a firefighter tell us how you apply principles of chemistry and physics of firefighting by explaining why you took each step. Explain the math formulas you used. Show us how you worked with witnesses to collect information, how you observed evidence, and how you worked with survivors in the aftermath. As you advanced in rank, tell how you responded to a similar event in a different way, perhaps more involved in the command structure or the management of people and materials.

Similarly, if you are an area planner or scheduler you can take one product or fixture and "walk through" the documentation of the manufacturing process. Describe the planning or scheduling database and write about the entire set of interactions with each of the departments and people involved in these processes. You may earn a variety of college course credits from one job task you performed if it crossed over into several different skills: managing, leading discussion groups, using planning software.

Each of your essays must contain this high level of detail because you are trying to earn the maximum number of college credits in the widest variety of classes and merit the highest grades as a result of your effort. Most Assessment of Prior Learning programs are associated with colleges that grant APL credits for courses as they are listed in the college catalog. If a course were listed as one in which a student would receive a letter grade (for example, A, B, C. or D) then you would be eligible to receive a grade as well as credit for the course.

As you make your academic plans you will want to apply for credit in areas outside your "major" field. If you are a firefighter, you may earn credits in firefighting. You may also earn credits in science, math and communication. Whatever your field, you may not be restricted to your "major" area because the actual experiences you have cross-over to many other fields that are taught at colleges. Your essay must represent these cross-over experiences in order for you to be considered for these credits.

Writing Style

Your Instructor may tell you that you need to revise your essay so that it reads more smoothly.

Copyright ©1980, 1999, 2001 Roslyn Snow

Smooth writing comes from using adequate transitions between thoughts in a paragraph and between paragraphs in the essay. You may have written your essay after you reviewed your resume or your job description and you copied those styles. Resumes and job descriptions do not use transitions. They are outlines and guide the reader from point to point by numbers or bullets. You need to guide the reader through an example or case history using **words** that specify time and place to make transitions: *First, second, third, before, after, during, while, for three days, there, here, on the second page, in the file cabinet, behind, across, on the next row, in the section on contracts.* Use these transitional words to begin sentences and to start paragraphs.

When you explain *why* you chose one option over another in your case history, you need language that specifies cause and effect, classification, definition, and other relationships. You need to use words that specify relationships between details, such as *if, then, because, as a result, depends on, in order to, except for, while, for this reason, similarly, a number of types, unlike.*

Handling Unpleasant Tasks

Most of your career experiences have been positive. Your essays reflect your career growth and what you have learned from your employers and organizations. At some point, however, you may have had a difficult time at work. You may have experienced personal harassment from a supervisor. You may have been promoted over more experienced (and resentful) co-workers. You may have had to discipline employees for personal reasons or for violations of company policy. You may have had a problem working for your manager or owner. You may have been helpless to respond to breach of company ethics on the part of an owner or manager. Your work decisions may have been challenged or opposed. Do you cover these incidents, and, if so, how?

If there was a lesson to be learned from the way you handled the difficult work situation, include it. Often these incidents make the best "case histories" in your essay. They allow you to analyze your ability to relate to people, to be firm in applying principles and policies, and yet flexible in structuring win-win solutions. Do not be reluctant to discuss work firings or demotions as long as you explain the circumstances in enough detail to understand how the problem arose and how you handled it.

Copyright ©1980, 1999, 2001 Roslyn Snow

As long as you try to find meaning and insight in the incident and do not use it to demean or express dissatisfaction or anger with an employer or co-worker, it will be relevant to your essay. Your APL Instructor will help you maintain an objective and positive point of view.

> Continue to send your essays about each position and job in your Chronology. Wait for comment from your Instructor before proceeding to a new essay. Save all of your work on your computer hard drive or disc.

Writing the Conclusion

When you have completed the essay segment about the last job you held or your current job, write a concluding paragraph that *reviews your career to date and then looks ahead to your future plans.* You need not mention every job you had in your concluding paragraph. However, it is a good idea to summarize the progress you have made over the years. If you went from machinist to program director, emphasize that achievement. If you started as a receptionist and now are a program administrator, be sure to make that point. If you began stocking shelves and bagging groceries and now are a store manager, this is the place to remind the reader of that progress. Then write about your plans for the future. When do you expect to receive your bachelor's degree, and what job title are you hoping to work toward next in your career?

> Send your concluding paragraph to your APL Instructor.

Exercise 3: EDUCATION AND TRAINING; LIFE EXPERIENCE

Prepare two new sections of your Portfolio Essay. This first is titled **Education and Training.** This section gives you an opportunity to elaborate on the workshops, seminars, in-service training sessions you may have taken at your company or at off-site locations. Describe in one or two short paragraphs what you learned and how the workshop was taught. Describe any assignments, tests, or projects you completed. Tell how you applied the instruction to your work or life. Use this format for your heading

Name of Workshop, Course or Seminar
Sponsoring Organization (school, your company trainer)
Dates Attended
Number of Hours
Topics Covered:

You are going to write about only those classes for which you have not received college credits. These will include company-sponsored courses, university extension, and non-accredited classes at proprietary or trade schools, Toastmasters, personal finance seminars, church related religious or Bible studies.

- Describe the topics covered and information presented in each class. Write in essay form. Do not copy information from the course brochure.

- Tell how the class was conducted. Was it a workshop, discussion, lecture, audio-visual presentation? Did you have homework, projects, and tests? Did you role-play or participate in discussions?

- What were the main skills you mastered?

- What concepts did you learn?

- What new procedures did you learn? What laws or regulations did you learn that affect your job?

- What presentation skills did you practice and learn?

Copyright ©1980, 1999, 2001 Roslyn Snow

Sample of Education and Training Essay

The Trainers' Program
Sponsored by: Computer Advisory Network (CAN)
October/November, 1999
Number of Hours: 39.0
Topics Covered:

This training program was held at a computer lab that had been set up at my employer's facility. This training program taught the use of personal computers, their programs and operating systems. This program was provided to employees who had been identified by their functional organization to become trainers in the use of personal computers throughout the facility. The training schedule included the following courses: Disk Operating System (DOS); Symphony I; Symphony II; WordPerfect I; WordPerfect II; Harvard Graphics, and Laser Printer Usage.

Each course was six hours with the exception of a three hour Laser Printer Usage course. During each of these courses we were trained at the computer keyboard. We were also provided with printed information relative to each of the software programs. This information was covered by the course instructor who lectured and illustrated his explanation via an overhead projector connected to his computer. There were hands-on assignments that we completed at our computer. The DOS segment covered the definition of DOS; review of RAM; hard and floppy disks.

Copyright ©1980, 1999, 2001 Roslyn Snow

LIFE EXPERIENCE

The second part of this exercise is to write about your personal, hobby, or community experiences. Adding this information "rounds out" the portrait of yourself. Experiences you enjoy on your own time involve skills taught in college classrooms. You may receive college credits for them if your background is sufficient. These experiences may add to or enrich the impression the evaluators have of you.

> These are some of the life experiences that may help you earn additional college credits.

Lessons in a dance or sport.

 A hobby such as painting or photography, flying a plane, acting in Community Theater.

 Inventing a product or process or running a business.

Volunteer work or public service.

Write a one- or two-page essay about each life experience. Choose recent experiences that you do regularly. These essays will be in a separate section of your Essay titled **Life Experience**. Title each separate essay with a heading, such as Sports, Theatrical Experience, Self-Improvement, or the company name you used in your own business.

Here are some helpful hints about writing these essays.

- ✓ Tell where and how long you studied folk dance, tennis, karate, aerobics. How often do you do this activity?

- ✓ What instrument do you play? Name some pieces you have mastered. Tell how often you play and what a typical session would include, such as scales, chord progressions, particular pieces you practice.

- ✓ Tell if you paint in oils, pastels, or watercolors? What subjects do you paint? Walk through one painting you completed telling us how you chose the subject and the artistic materials.

- ✓ Did you serve on a committee or hold an office? Did you conduct meetings, give speeches, and collect contributions, tutor, or coach children? Walk through one committee meeting in which you contributed to the decisions that were made.

- ✓ What self-improvement program did you complete? EST? Lifespring? Dale Carnegie? Marriage Encounter? Walk through one session telling what problems or weaknesses you discovered and steps you took to improve or enrich your business or personal life.

- ✓ What business did you own and operate? Describe all the steps you took to open your business or practice, such as permits, license, tax ID number, and fictitious name. Tell what bookkeeping system you used. Tell what marketing techniques you found useful. If your business is no longer current tell how you closed it.

- ✓ What product or process did you invent? Tell what legal steps you took to protect your interest in it. Tell how your product or process worked. Tell what has happened to your product or process since you invented it.

Send your Education and Training and Life Experience essays to your Instructor now.

Copyright ©1980, 1999, 2001 Roslyn Snow

Portfolio Essay

Now that you have added your Education and Training and Life Experience essays, use this checklist to review the work you have done.

☐ Have you added HEADINGS to each essay? Each new job or job position, each training seminar or course, and each life experience segment must have a separate HEADING.

☐ Have you used essay form in writing each essay? Do not use bulleted lists or sentence fragments taken from your career resume. You must have complete sentences and paragraphs in each essay.

☐ Have you kept all of your writing in PAST TENSE except for those activities you are doing currently?

☐ How many pages have you written? If your Portfolio Essay contains fewer than 30 pages, ask your Instructor to review it at this time to make sure you have adequate detail and examples. Your Instructor may not have noticed missing explanations or "walk throughs," especially if there were interruptions during the time you wrote your essays. You may have left out some pages when you printed your essays. Go no further until your Instructor has approved your entire Portfolio Essay.

☐ Have you explained HOW you perform each activity you include in each essay, including life experience essays?

☐ Have you backed up all of your computer files or printed a hard copy of your Portfolio Essay? Remember, your Instructor will not keep copies of your work. You must protect your Portfolio Essay files.

Copyright ©1980, 1999, 2001 Roslyn Snow

Exercise 4: The INTRODUCTION

The last exercise in your Portfolio will be the first the evaluators will see when your Portfolio is compiled. Write it exactly as you see it here, filling in the blanks as indicated.

There are five components to cover in writing your one page **Introduction:**

- ❏ **Title your page.** INTRODUCTION

- ❏ **State your educational goal.** The learning I have acquired will allow me to meet the requirements for (the Associate in Arts degree in general studies or transfer to a four-year college). As I continue my studies, I hope to earn a Bachelor of Arts degree in _____ from _____ _____ University.

- ❏ **State your career goal.** After receiving my degree, I will continue at my present job, but my chances for promotion will be enhanced.

- ❏ **Tell how you intend to reach your goal.** I am enrolled at (or enrolling at) _____ College or University where I will take the units necessary to complete my degree.

- ❏ **Tell where you acquired your prior learning.** I am asking for credit for learning I acquired on-the-job, through adult education courses, training courses, and seminars and in life.

> Send your Education and Training and Life Experience essays to your Instructor now.

Copyright ©1980, 1999, 2001 Roslyn Snow

CONGRATULATIONS!

You have now completed your Portfolio Essay. You have written all three sections: *Work Experience, Education and Training, and Life Experience.* You have written your *Introduction.* You have completed over 90 percent of the task of creating your Portfolio.

Where Do You Go From Here?

Before you can convince the college faculty evaluators that you have the knowledge to earn college credits, you need to show them samples of your work. You will need both samples of work you have completed on the job as well as other documents that follow your work trail, so to speak, such as letters from employers and co-workers, minutes from meetings you attend, correspondence that shows your involvement in work projects, charts, drawings, spreadsheets, flyers, ads, photos showing work you created. This will give you an opportunity to *showcase* your portfolio essays, to display the best examples of your work, the accomplishments of which you are the most proud.

Chapter Three: Documenting the Essay

You are well on your way to creating a career album that will portray your work and life experience history. You have written about how you have performed each of the jobs you have had and what you have accomplished in your career.

Now you will create a showcase for your essays by choosing documents that show what you have achieved.

Exercise 5: WRITING SOLICITATION LETTERS

The most important documents will be letters from employers, co-workers, and colleagues. Choose as many as nine or 10 people who can *testify* to many of the statements you made in your essay about your work accomplishments and your life achievements.

Do not look at these letters as job verifications or reference letters. Solicit a detailed response by sending a **solicitation letter.**

Write letters to each of your employers and working colleagues asking them to verify the experiences you wrote about in your essays. Follow the **sample solicitation letter** as a model. You must be very detailed in these letters. You want the response to be a letter that echoes what you wrote in your essay. You want your letter writer to comment on the duties you wrote about, the projects that you completed and your accomplishments. Spotlight the duties you performed and the projects you completed in your solicitation letter. Do *not* send a copy of your essays to your letter writer.

You may write to more than one supervisor or co-worker at each company. Perhaps you report to more than one supervisor. Perhaps several letters will be needed to verify all aspects of your job duties.

Attach a **guideline letter** to each solicitation letter you send. The guideline letters should be on your college's stationery.

Copyright ©1980, 1999, 2001 Roslyn Snow

Re-read your essay segments carefully before you write your solicitation letter so that you have lists of points that you have included in your essays: job duties, job analyses, anecdotes, examples, illustrations. In brief form, list the duties and accomplishments that each letter writer would best remember.

You do not want letters that merely verify your employment. You want letters from people who can testify to the job analyses and anecdotes you wrote in your essay segments. For that reason your solicitation letters are crucial to this part of the portfolio process because they highlight exactly what you want your letter writer to say.

Your solicitation letter should jog the memory of the letter writer. You should remind them of your responsibilities when you worked for or with them. You should remind them of your accomplishments. If you saved money on purchasing or increased productivity or hired excellent workers, mention these accomplishments. If there were specific outcomes to your employment, such as designs you created, prototypes you built, homes you sold, mention these.

It is important to send many different letters. No one employer or co-worker will remember everything you did. Each letter writer will have different memories and a different perspective on your work.

Send solicitation letters to:

- ✓ Employers, managers, supervisors

- ✓ Co-workers

- ✓ Clients

- ✓ Workers in other companies you did business with such as vendors or suppliers

- ✓ Seminar trainers and other teachers

Copyright ©1980, 1999, 2001 Roslyn Snow

- ✓ People connected to your community activities such as coaches, social service agencies

- ✓ People connected to your self-employment activities such as your bookkeeper, realtor, customers

Keep a log of all solicitation letters you sent so you can track the responses as they arrive. If possible, telephone the letter writers in advance so that they will be expecting this request.

If you know the letter writer well, ask for a copy of the response to be sent to you so you do not have to wait for your APL Instructor to send it to you. Include self-addressed and stamped envelopes to hasten the reply.

> **CAUTION**

You may be apprehensive about receiving a letter from an employer from an early job. Perhaps the company no longer exists or the management no longer remembers your services. Do not let that fear stop you from sending out a solicitation letter. Our experience has shown that letters often appear from employers that you think you cannot locate.

> Send your letters to your APL Instructor now. Do *not* mail your letters until your Instructor has approved them.

SAMPLE SOLICITATION LETTER

Date
Mr. John Manager, Branch Manager
XYZ Company
111 First St.
Copely, CA 99999

Dear Mr. Manager:

I am enrolled in a college program that matches learning acquired on-the-job with academic units. I have written about my experience at XYZ in support of my petition for college credits in business **(YOU MAY INSERT INSTEAD YOUR MAJOR FIELD, SUCH AS HEALTH SCIENCE, COMMUNICATION, OR TECHNOLOGY)**. In my essay, I have made certain statements about my responsibilities in your department. I am requesting that you verify these statements in your own words.

Here are some of the specific statements I would like you to verify and comment on in a letter to the college.

■ During my employment, I developed the five-minute trouble shooting procedure using the K-tran tool to identify faulty circuits. The procedure was expanded and written up for use nationally.
I developed a plan for using Western Union Operator 25 and to consolidate seven area offices throughout the 11 regional areas into one central station.

■ I developed and printed the first Zip Code Service Directory for the Western Area that was later used nationally.

■ I attended the K-T Training School in Wichita on assignment from your department. I completed a five-day training in supervision conducted by the University of Nebraska in connection with my duties as leadsman.

I have enclosed a guideline the college has provided that explains the program and the purpose of the letter you are writing. Please address your reply and return this letter to **(INSERT THE NAME OF YOUR APL INSTRUCTOR, THE SCHOOL, AND SCHOOL ADDRESS HERE)**.

Sincerely,
(Signed)
Your name
Address
City, State Zip
Phone Number
Enclosures: College Guideline; self-addressed, stamped envelope

Copyright ©1980, 1999, 2001 Roslyn Snow

SAMPLE GUIDELINE LETTER

Your APL Instructor will mail you several guideline letters to attach to your solicitation letters.

Your College Letterhead
Your College or Institution Address, Telephone and E-Mail Address

---

Dear Friend:

You have been asked to write a letter in support of a candidate who is seeking college credit for prior learning. The Assessment of Prior Learning Program at *Name of Institution* offers the opportunity to receive college credits for learning acquired outside of the classroom, on the job or through company-sponsored training. Your letter will help the faculty evaluators understand the specific job tasks the candidate performed, the projects worked on and accomplished and the training completed.

Please use letterhead stationery if available. Tell something of your present position and the position you held when you knew the candidate. In verifying the candidate's work experience, tell something of the major responsibilities, tasks performed and projects completed in the course of employment or other association. If you remember specific anecdotes involving the candidate's job performance, please include them.

Your letter will be added to the candidate's Portfolio. You may send the candidate a copy of your letter for this purpose. The original should be sent to me. We thank you for taking time to provide as thoughtful and candid a reply as possible.

Sincerely,

Name of Instructor,

Name of Institution

Copyright ©1980, 1999, 2001 Roslyn Snow

Sending Solicitation Letters

> Your Instructor has reviewed your previous assignment. If you needed to make any changes or revisions, your Instructor has told you
>
> ■ You may have written the same solicitation letter to a variety of previous employers or co-workers. Your instructor will remind you that each letter must address different facets of your job that only the letter-writer would be able to comment on.
>
> ■ You may have sent your instructor only one solicitation letter to review. Your instructor needs to see all of your letters at one time to determine if you are covering all of the skills and knowledge that you have written about in your essay. Wait until all your letters are written. Send them to your instructor **before** sending them to your employers or co-workers.
>
> ■ You may have placed the items to be verified within the paragraphs of your letter. It is better to highlight your duties, projects, and accomplishments by indenting them, using numbers or bullets to set them off. You may have been asked to do this.

Often students will list job duties, as on a resume. It is better to use first person "I" statements: <u>I</u> led the meetings of the quality committee, or <u>I</u> gave the new employee orientation presentation.

Often students will ask the employer to comment about their work in general. It is better to identify five or six duties, responsibilities, projects, or accomplishments that the respondent can verify.

Before you move on to a new milestone in your APL Portfolio project, be sure that you have asked for letters from employers, work colleagues, trainers, teachers, and people you have worked with in your jobs and life experiences.

Your letters are not only proof. They are testimony. They will create an impression in the minds of your evaluators if they are current, unique and detailed.

Exercise 6: Documents and Document Signals

What Documents Should You Showcase?

There are many ways to verify the learning experiences you have related in your Portfolio Essay. Here is a checklist of documents you should look for among your papers at work and at home.

- ❏ Work samples: reports, charts, letters you wrote, forms you created, designs, schematics, codes or laws you follow, budgets, accounting ledgers and journals, financial statements, proposals

- ❏ Performance reviews, promotions or status changes

- ❏ Licenses, certificates and awards

- ❏ In-service or private course outlines or brochures

Copyright ©1980, 1999, 2001 Roslyn Snow

- ☐ Clippings and photos; cassette tapes or CDs of your performances

- ☐ Letters from teachers or friends relating to hobbies or sports or private instruction

- ☐ Diplomas or transcripts from non-accredited schools

Work Sample Documents

The most important type of document to include is the **work sample** document. If you have been a "pack rat" throughout your working years, this will be easy. You have filing cabinets filled with samples of work you produced. If you have not kept a file from previous jobs, you will have problems in this assignment. You might want to meet with a former employer or co-worker and ask if he or she would be willing to give you copies of documents that you worked on, or documents that represent work similar to what you did.

You should have no fewer than **10 work sample** documents.

Most of these work samples will be from your current job. You may conceal names and other confidential or proprietary information. Choose the most complex, the longest, the most fully developed, and the most excellent work samples you can find.

Do not put in 10 samples of the same type of work product. Find different products to share: letters, reports, forms you created, designs you drafted, blueprints of parts you manufactured, contracts you developed, floor plans for moving equipment or office furniture, flyers, brochures, briefing visuals you created, photos of machine parts you produced or of your work space. On each document note the type of equipment used to produce the sample (I created this advertising brochure using Microsoft Publisher).

Performance Reviews

A second important type of document is **the performance review.** You should have no fewer than three performance reviews or evaluations. Try to get at least **three reviews** from **different** job positions. More is better.

Other Documents

Licenses, certificates, and awards should match activities you wrote about in your Portfolio Essay. If you find a license or certificate or award that you did not write about, *add the information to your essay now* if it represents an activity you have done recently.

Include **notes and outlines** for speeches or presentations you gave.

Clippings and photos may be used if they document accomplishments on the job, such as write-ups in business magazines or photos of some of the hobby items you created. Letters from friends and teachers may also help document hobbies, sports or private instruction, such as music or flying.

Course outlines and brochures will help the evaluators understand what was taught in the seminars and courses you attended. Remember, only non-accredited courses are included in your Portfolio. Use outlines and brochures from non-accredited courses only.

Include **homework assignments, lecture notes, or tests** you took in your training classes.

Include **diplomas and transcripts** from non-accredited schools *only*. While you will not receive college credits automatically for the non-accredited school courses you have taken, they will become part of your evaluation and may help you receive college credits.

You will *not* present transcripts from fully accredited schools you attended as documents in your Portfolio. You have already received college credits for these courses. They are already on your official records and will be considered for transfer by the college or university of your choice.

Copyright ©1980, 1999, 2001 Roslyn Snow

More About... Collecting Documents

1. List the **responses to your solicitation letters.**

    It may be too early for you to have received all of your responses. However, you have a list of the solicitation letters you sent. Follow up by telephone to determine which of your letter writers will respond. Some students use a blank page to substitute for the letter they hope to receive. List response letters by name of letter writer, and name of company. Later you will add a Document Number.

2. Collect **work samples**, such as

    - Letters and reports you have written
    - Spreadsheets or database records that you have processed, especially from your most current jobs
    - Forms you created or used
    - Graphics charts you designed or processed
    - Databases you monitored
    - Minutes from meetings you attended that show your participation
    - Letters from customers or co-workers that show your involvement with projects or your handling of responsibilities
    - Pictures of you on the job

You should be able to present at least 10 samples of your own work. Include as many as possible. More is better.

3.   Collect **performance reviews**.

4.   Collect **other documents:**

- Copies of the syllabus and course outlines, notes you took, handouts you received, and assignments you completed from training classes you attended
- Pictures or clippings and other records relating to the life experiences you wrote about in your essay
- Tax records and other business documents for self-employment; budgets, or credit documents for personal life management; journals, and self-study notes for personal improvement
- Video or audiocassettes that demonstrate speech or musical presentations
- Portfolio objects to demonstrate creative artwork, such as jewelry, painting, drawing, and ceramics
- High-quality photographs to show works of art if you do not have originals.

Copyright ©1980, 1999, 2001 Roslyn Snow

Choosing Your Documents

Use the following checklist to be sure you have chosen the most effective documents to include in your portfolio.

- [ ] Have you found at least three performance reviews from jobs you have held?

- [ ] Have you found at least 10 samples of work you did in your job positions?

- [ ] Have you found documents related to your training, such as lecture notes, homework, tests, brochures, and handouts?

- [ ] Have you found documents related to hobbies or private instruction, such as flying logs, samples of jewelry you made, programs from recitals or concerts?

- [ ] Have you found documents related to your life experiences such as photos and clippings and legal, tax and accounting records from any of your businesses?

How Do You Organize Your Documents?

Very soon your letters will start coming in. Make a list of those letters you expect to receive. There may be just one or two letters you are not sure of.

You can begin to organize your documents.

Put the letters you have received in a separate file. Add to the file a blank "holding sheet" for each letter you believe you will receive, even if the letter has not yet arrived.

Add the work-related documents to this file.

Put all of the documents related to training and life experience in a separate file.

Organize the Documents Within Each File

Go through each file and organize the documents in chronological order. Organize one file at a time.

- ✓ Sort the letters and work related documents in chronological order.
- ✓ Sort the training documents in chronological order.
- ✓ Sort the life experience documents in chronological order.

How Do You Number and Name Your Documents?

Number each document starting with **101**. Assign a number to the letters you expect to receive, even if you do not have them now. Use a light pencil or non-stick label to number each document so you can keep the original in neat and clean condition.

Make a *list* of all of the documents by number starting with 101 and by descriptor The *descriptor* will be the *name* you give each document. It may be "Sample of Departmental Budget I Submitted for Approval." It may be "Photo Showing Window Display I Created." Or it may be "Blueprints Showing List of Materials and Cuts for Hex Nut I Designed."

Copyright ©1980, 1999, 2001 Roslyn Snow

Document Signals

Place your portfolio essays on your worktable, next to your list of documents and the documents themselves. As you turn the pages of your essays, match each document to events or activities you wrote about in the essay. At each match point, insert a **document signal** by placing the document number in parenthesis **(Document 101)** within the paragraph that the document illustrates or references.

This is similar to inserting footnotes within a term paper or research paper.

For instance, a performance appraisal from your very first employer, 20 years ago, might be the only document that matches the events or job duties you described in your first essay. You have numbered the performance appraisal Document 101. Place the document signal (Document 101) in the first paragraph of that essay near the description of the work experience you are documenting.

Your next document may be a letter you are expecting from the employer you mentioned in your third essay. You may not have the letter yet, but you spoke with this person and you are sure that you will receive it. Use a blank piece of paper to *substitute* for this letter until it arrives. Number that letter Document 102. Write the document number on the substitute and insert the signal (Document 102) within the first or second paragraph of this essay.

There may be some early jobs for which you have no documents. In the example above, for instance, you do not have a document for your second essay. The faculty evaluators will understand that you cannot produce documents for each job, especially those you held early in your career. They will evaluate your documents on the basis of a *preponderance* of documentation. They will expect you to have documents from your recent jobs, and, particularly, work sample documents from your current job.

Go through each of your documents, matching the documents to your job story as best you can. You will not have a perfect match, but you will have documents that speak in your behalf or demonstrate the type of work you have described. You are creating a *showcase* for your documents by relating them to what you wrote in your Portfolio Essay.

You will place all of the documents at the back section of your Portfolio when you have completed this project. We will show you how to assemble all the parts of your Portfolio, including the section where the original documents will be placed. For now, keep your documents in a clean, safe place.

Copyright ©1980, 1999, 2001 Roslyn Snow

STUDENT ESSAY PAGE SAMPLE WITH DOCUMENT SIGNAL

I kept personnel folders on each employee in the group. The folders were set up in a format according to company guidelines. **(Document 103)** I maintained the folders in a secure cabinet. As various documents were received, I filed them in the appropriate section of the personnel folder. I had to make sure that the folders were accounted because they were confidential. I was allowed to provide them to specific members of management for review.

I prepared and typed Employee Change Notices if an employee in the group was due to receive a merit increase or a promotion. **(Document 104)** The five-part form contained pre-printed information such as employee name, Social Security number, current classification code and title, and current rate of pay. I calculated the increase and new rate of pay. I used a specific calculation to convert the new monthly base salary into an hourly figure.

How the Document Showcase Works

The faculty evaluator can see your **document signals in parentheses** in your essay. At any time the evaluator can turn to the back section of your Portfolio and see the actual document numbered Document 104. In this case, the document is an Employee Change Notice that the student prepared.

Send your APL Instructor a page from your work experience essay showing how you have inserted the **Document Signals** within your text.

Copyright ©1980, 1999, 2001 Roslyn Snow

Organizing Documents

Put all the documents, *including the letters you are expecting*, in the order mentioned in the essays: jobs, training, and life experience.

1. **Number** each document.
2. **Mark** the document with its number.
3. **Insert document signals** within the essay.

Picture this: You are at home at your kitchen table or workbench. You have your essays on one side and all of your documents on another. As you turn the pages of your essay, choose documents that reflect, demonstrate, prove, or showcase what you have said on that essay page. Your first document may be a W-2, proving you worked at a company long ago, perhaps no longer in existence. It may be the only documentation you could get for this experience. *Mark* DOCUMENT 101 in pencil on the upper right hand corner of the document. *Insert a signal* (Document 101) at the end of the first sentence or the first paragraph in your essay that indicates you worked at this company or organization.

Your next document may also be a W-2. Many students find themselves unable to document the very earliest jobs in any other manner. Sometimes they cannot even find a W-2.

However, as you turn the pages of your essay, you will soon come to jobs for which you do have one or two documents. Your next document may be a letter from an employer that you are sure you will receive. You may also have a performance review or a copy of your job duties. You may even have an early work sample. Again, number these documents in order, Document 102 or 103 or 104. Insert the signal in your essay immediately so that

Copyright ©1980, 1999, 2001 Roslyn Snow

you can match the passage in the essay with the document. You may not have the exact spreadsheet you wrote about, for example, but it is a Lotus 1-2-3 spreadsheet and illustrates your performance capabilities.

As you move along, you will find more spaces within essay passages in which to insert letters from employers that you expect to receive and more samples of your own work.

It is a good idea to insert the *document signal* for a letter from an employer in the first paragraph of an essay segment, when you mention you were first hired or first promoted.

Match the work samples with passages in your essay that describe that kind of work: speech presentations with copies of view graphs or PowerPoint documents; inputting and formatting correspondence with samples of letters you wrote or prepared from notes or rough draft.

Add your training and life experience documents. Your training documents will follow your job documents. Your life experience documents will be last.

At this point, you have completed your document numbering system. Each document is numbered. You have completed the most difficult part of this project by indexing each document to the essay section it best illustrates and inserting key document signals. This will help you *showcase* your essays by giving the faculty evaluators a chance to see

- How you describe the work you did
- What employers and co-workers have said about your work
- Samples of the work itself

Copyright ©1980, 1999, 2001 Roslyn Snow

> Re-Submit one essay page to your APL Instructor showing how you have inserted *document signals*.

Exercise 7: INDEX TO DOCUMENTS

Keep a log of your Documents. Assign a number to each document and list the document by number and by name. The name of the document is its *descriptor* or *annotation*. The log will be your **Index to Documents**.

✓ Use descriptive and action words for each document annotation. (Past Due Notice Form **I** Created) so that the reader can tell what the document is and what *your relationship* to it is. Did you create the document? Did you write it? Did you compute the formulas it uses? Did you draw it? Did you negotiate it?

✓ Use only portions of your documents that show *your work*. Do not include pages of course outlines, brochures, manuals or advertising materials that describe your company, product or training. Include only those parts that show your role or function and show your original work. Be sure to put the **"I"** statement on your annotation of each document that represents a sample of your own work.

✓ Excerpt from long multi-page materials rather than including the entire document, even if you wrote or prepared the whole document. Use two or three pages only. If you are including a syllabus or training manual, use only the table of contents, index and sample pages, especially those showing assignments. Tell the number of pages of the original document. For instance:
Document 140 Shareholders Report Excerpt 10/243 pages.

✓ Use long multi-page or oversized materials only if the production or presentation of the document shows your unique work in graphics or presentation format, as in a published book or a portfolio of drawings or blueprints. Plan to place these materials in a separate binder. Indicate this on your Index to Documents:
Document 141 My Charcoal Drawings; See Separate Binder.

Copyright ©1980, 1999, 2001 Roslyn Snow

STUDENT SAMPLE

(The identity of managers and other employers and companies are not given on this student sample. You will include all names of letter writers, employers, co-workers, companies and organizations on your Index to Documents. You will also include the work titles of all managers and supervisors.)

INDEX TO DOCUMENTS

101. Performance Appraisal, Lev Furniture, Jim W.

102. W-2 Form, Decorator Ind, Miami, Florida

103. Individual Tax Form, Decorator Industries

104. Letter, Russ W., American Bankers Co,

105. Letter, Monica W., Southern Bell Telephone Company

106. Sample of Requisition I input into AIMS system

107. Letter, Jim S., Procurement Manager

108. Sample Debit Memo I processed

109. Sample of Request for Information I completed

110. Procedure for incoming calls

111. Performance Review 10/29/85, Account Clerk Sr

112. Filenet 3270 Introduction and Procedures

113. Instruction I use to open a Batch M&D System

114. Process I inputted for entering invoices

115. Performance Review, Account Clerk Sr, 9/9/87

116. Letter, Mary O., Supervisor, Northrop

117. Performance Review, Account Clerk Spec, 4/28/88

Copyright ©1980, 1999, 2001 Roslyn Snow

118. Procedure I used for Progress Payments
119. Sample of Payment Process I input
120. Sample of Invoice Approval Routing Sheet I wrote
121. Sample of Liquidation Invoice I processed
122. Sample of Paid Invoices I posted
123. Sample of Check Analysis Sheet I processed
124. Letter, Teresa M., Major Subcontracts
125. Certificate of Appreciation, Kevin J., Manager
126. Procedure of Invoice Approval using M&D
127. Certificate of Appreciation, John A., Manager
128. Sample of Invoice Status Charts I set up,
129. Performance Reviews, 2/26/90 and 1/8/91
130. Samples of My Cash Forecasting
131. Sample Forecasting Requirements I completed
132. Letter, Gerald A., Month End Closing
133. Performance Review, 11/19/92
134. Sample of Spreadsheet I designed for Variances
135. Sample of Journal I processed monthly
136. Sample of Journal and Spreadsheet I processed
137. Performance Reviews, 12/17/93, 12/19/94
138. Record Sheet of Company Training Classes I Attended
139. McCormack and Dodge Millennium Training
140. Certificate -- Spreadsheets and Graphics
141. Certificate of Completion Total Quality Mgmt
142. Certificate of Completion Communication Women

Copyright ©1980, 1999, 2001 Roslyn Snow

143. Course Content Presentation Skills and Critique

144. Course Content Introduction to Word

145. Course Content -- Introduction to PowerPoint

146. Certificate of Completion -- Manage Priorities

147. Certificate of Completion -- Assertive Skills For Women

148. Letter, Rachel K. from the San Bernardino Mayor's office concerning Sister City Exchange Students, 12/30/94

149. Newspaper clippings from the Los Angeles Times and San Gabriel Tribune on BKK Evacuations and Problems, 1998.

The Document Labels

Place all of your documents at the back of your Portfolio in a separate **document section**. You have already made a list or Index to Documents showing the document number and descriptor or annotation.

Each document will be labeled with its Document Number and name or annotation on the upper right hand corner of the first page of the document.

Create a label file on your computer from your Index to Documents. Using a label template in your word processing program, format your Index so that you can print individual labels for each entry on the Index. Some students create a database so that they can use the mail merge function in Word or WordPerfect. In this way, you can include the entire document annotation. You may find a simpler or different way to do this, but you must have *each document labeled and annotated.*

If you cannot make a computer label, type the document labels. Do not hand write them. It is all right if you cover up some of the text or graphics on your document when you paste the label on the first page of the document.

Copyright ©1980, 1999, 2001 Roslyn Snow

Sample Document Showing Label and Annotation

Document label

Document 129
Cost Analysis I Performed

Company X – Organization Y*
Planning Level
Cost Estimate

Capital Expenses:	Diesel	Propane	Electric
1 Generator Purchase	$ 45,000.00	$230,000.00	
2 Electrical Line Installation			$250,000.00
Environmental Credit			$ (15,000.00)
3 Fuel Tank Purchase	$ 17,500.00	$ 23,000.00	
Includes Delivery, Slab,			
Installation and Piping			
4 Average Pollution Control Cost	$227,000.00		
Contingency	$ 32,000.00	$26,000.00	$ 21,000.00
Total:	$321,500.00	$279,000.00	$256,000.00

* Company names are not identified in this text. Your document may identify the companies or organizations involved. You can conceal any proprietary information you wish.

Documentation

Use the following checklist to be sure you have completed your Index to Documents and document signals.

- [ ] Have you sorted the work experience documents chronologically?
- [ ] Have you sorted the training and life experience documents chronologically?
- [ ] Have you numbered these documents in order starting with Document 101?
- [ ] Have you included those letters you expect to receive so you can track their return?
- [ ] Have you inserted the document numbers, **document signals**, within the paragraphs to which they relate in your essays?
- [ ] Have you created a **Document Index** by number and name or annotation?
- [ ] Have you placed the number and annotation on the upper right hand corner of the first page of each document using a word processing **label** program?

> Send your **Index to Documents** and a copy of one of your documents showing your **document label** to your APL Instructor. Wait until you have this assignment approved before going to the next.

Your Index to Documents

Your Instructor will review your Index to Documents with an eye to the course credits you will be requesting. The documents you have included along with the detail in your essays will determine the courses you will request for credit. This is the time to re-examine your Index to Documents.

■ You may not have listed the letters you are expecting from work colleagues, employers and others. List these letters now so you will not have to re-organize your documents at a later time.

■ You may have listed your solicitation letters in your Index. List *only* the response from the employer, work colleague or other letter writer.

■ You may not have enough work sample documents. You should have at least 10 examples of your own work representing such areas as correspondence, reports, computer software use, program management, presentations, designs, or forms you created.

■ You may not have named your work sample documents. Without a document name or annotation that tells that you prepared, created, wrote, typed, keyed, drew, or supervised the creation of the document, the evaluators will not know why it is in your Portfolio. Caption each work sample by writing a first person "I" statement telling what you did to prepare the document.

Chapter Four: Choosing Transferable Credits

Your Instructor has arranged for you to receive a **college catalog** from the admissions office of the accredited college that will evaluate your portfolio. You will prepare a **Request for Credit**, listing the courses in the catalog you wish to have granted through your portfolio assessment.

How Will You Know Which Course Credits To Request?

Your Request for Credit will be based on what you have written in your essays. You cannot receive college credits in courses in which you have not had experience and therefore have little knowledge.

We will help you by giving you guidelines to follow in choosing courses that will jump-start your education at the college or university of your choice.

Your APL Instructor will prepare a comprehensive Educational Plan that will list courses you need to meet degree requirements or transfer to a bachelor's degree program at an accredited college or university of your choice.

Copyright ©1980, 1999, 2001 Roslyn Snow

What If You Have Not Chosen a College or University Degree Program?

These are the best of times for working adults who want to return to school for an academic degree. Many fully accredited colleges and universities in almost all of the 50 states have programs designed for adults. These programs are known as **external degree programs.** They differ from regular degree programs in these ways:

1. Courses may be held at campus centers, usually close to work sites or even at work sites.
2. Courses may be held evenings or weekends.
3. Instruction is accelerated and courses shortened in length.
4. Instruction may make use of Internet and other technologies so that course work may be completed at home.
5. Faculty serves as mentors and facilitators rather than as lecturers.
6. Assessment of Prior Learning credits are accepted.
7. Learning assignments may be relevant to skills and concepts needed at work.

A good place to start looking for college and university programs is the reference, *External Degrees in the Information Age: Legitimate Choices* by Sullivan, Stewart and Spille, published by Oryx Press.

Your APL Instructor will be able to help recommend schools in your local area.

What Is An Accredited College or University?

Colleges and universities are part of an elaborate system of postsecondary education in the United States. They may be public or private institutions, for-profit or non-profit. The state in which they operate may have a licensing or registration procedure by statute. They may be allowed to advertise that they are an "approved" or "registered" institution.

Copyright ©1980, 1999, 2001 Roslyn Snow

However, they may not be fully accredited.

Accreditation is granted to colleges and universities whose programs and degree requirements are monitored by an accrediting body. There are

- National Institutional Accrediting Bodies that monitor specialized schools, such as trade and technical schools or seminaries
- Professional Accrediting Bodies that monitor professional instruction in such areas as law, health science, journalism, oriental medicine and psychology.
- Regional Institutional Accrediting Bodies that monitor accredited, degree-granting colleges and universities throughout the country.

When we advise you to attend only a fully accredited school, we mean a school that has been accredited by one of the Regional Institutional Accrediting Bodies:

- Middle States Association of Colleges and Schools (MSA)
- New England Association of Schools and Colleges (NEASC-CIHE)
- North Central Association of Colleges and Schools (NCA)
- The Northwest Association of Schools and Colleges (NASC)
- Southern Association of Colleges and Schools (SACS-CC)
- Western Association of Schools and Colleges Sr (WASC-Sr)

A college degree from a school approved by one of these accrediting bodies is a minimum requirement of acceptance into a graduate school or professional school program. Many employers will reimburse for your educational expenses only if you attend an accredited school. Many grants and scholarships or other financial aids depend on your attending an accredited school.

An accredited school will require that all credits you transfer be also from an accredited school. It is critical that you work with an accredited school to gain your APL credits. Otherwise they will not transfer to an accredited college or university.

Copyright ©1980, 1999, 2001 Roslyn Snow

Exercise 8: REQUEST FOR CREDIT

Your APL Instructor should make certain that the college evaluating your portfolio is fully accredited. When you receive the college catalog, look for the statement of accreditation, usually in the first two or three pages of the catalog.

Turn to the section of your college catalog entitled "Courses" or "Instruction." Here you will find descriptions of each course offered by the college in every academic department beginning with Accounting and ending in Welding Technology or Zoology.

Each course offered by the college has a **number:**
Mathematics 100 or Mathematics 1A
And a **name:**
Elementary Algebra.

The catalog includes a brief statement about the course content. You can get a good idea of the topics covered and the level of work required by reading this description

Here is a description of a course numbered Electronics Technology 170, named Electronic Construction Techniques:

Electronics Technology 170---Electronic Construction Techniques (3)
Recommended preparation: Electronics Technology 155 or 180, or concurrent enrollment.

Skill development in the areas of safety, recognition, and reading of various schematic, writing and servicing diagrams, component familiarization and testing, use of hand tools as they apply to soldering, desoldering, wiring and electronic assembly, use of equipment to test and troubleshoot electronic circuitry. Students are provided the opportunity to incorporate all these skills in the building of a final project that involves printed circuit board assembly, testing, troubleshooting and packaging. Student must furnish safety glasses. Two hours lecture, four hours laboratory. Offered: F; S.

The catalog entry includes the number of in-class hours a resident student would spend. From this number, the unit value is derived. For instance, a lecture class meeting one hour a week for 18 weeks (a semester) earns one credit or unit. Units are offered in multiples: 54 hours (3 hours weekly)= three units. Laboratory hours are usually computed at less than full value.

This course description lists the skills that students taking this course will develop and the tools and equipment they will use. From this description you can tell if you have written about similar skills and equipment. If so, you may want to request this course.

How Do You Choose Courses for Your Request for Credit?

Read the course descriptions in the section titled "Courses" or "Instruction" in the college catalog your APL Instructor will send you.

Choose no more than 20 college courses in which you feel you have knowledge as a result of experiences you described in your essays. Do not include accredited courses you have already completed at a college or university.

The course description printed in the college catalog should help you understand what skills and concepts are taught in each course, as well as typical assignments given. For instance, the course description for an Early Childhood Development course for parents may indicate that students will have active participation with their children in a preschool setting. A dBase4 course description may indicate a student will write programs to generate custom screens and custom reports.

Choose courses that you feel you have knowledge in as a result of your work experience, training, and life experience. *Do not choose courses based on college requirements at this time. Your APL Instructor will review your educational plan, and help you prepare a final draft of your Request for Credit.*

Be careful not to list courses in areas you enjoy but have no current experience. You may have played a musical instrument as a child, but can no longer read music and follow a score. You may be interested in Civil War history or the discoveries of the Dead Sea Scrolls, but you may not have had a guided activity in which the historical concepts have been discussed in a systematic way and a variety of opinions have been explored.

Copyright ©1980, 1999, 2001 Roslyn Snow

Stay close to what you know, to learning you have experienced, and to skills and concepts you have written about and documented. Trust your APL Instructor to help you modify or expand your list as your educational plans become clear.

Search the catalog for those courses you feel your experience qualifies you to receive through APL. The description will tell you what skills, concepts, and activities are presented in each course. If you have written about experiences in which you performed similar skills, used the same concepts and completed similar activities, add the course to your Request for Credit.

Concentrate on these areas: English, business, management, speech, and the technical areas of your experience, such as computer office technology, office information services, computer information services, drafting technology, machine technology, aviation services, welding, electronics technology, web technology and design, and health services.

These courses teach vocational or job-related skills and will be a good match for the work experiences you have written about in your essays.

Guidelines for Your Catalog Search:

- ✓ Ask your Instructor how many units you are limited to and *be sure to ask for more than that maximum number.*

- ✓ Request only those courses which teach material in which you have actual experience that has been guided by a trainer or occurred during your career in a work environment.

- ✓ Request those courses to which most of your documents relate; if you have many work samples showing your use of various word processing software, ask for all of the word processing classes that apply; if you have performance reviews and letters commending you on your ability to solve problems with difficult employees, ask for management communication, interpersonal communication and group dynamics classes.

- ✓ Do *not* request courses in which you have an interest or love (theater, literature, science) but no guided activities.

Copyright ©1980, 1999, 2001 Roslyn Snow

✓ Request courses that reflect your hobbies and life experience only if you can document them.

✓ Do not request remedial courses (designated 00 or an N).

List each course in alphabetical order by academic area or department and by:

Course number	Name	Units
Electronics 170	Construction Techniques	3.0
Math 130	Finite Math	4.0
Speech 114	Conducting Meetings	2.0
Technology 100	Innovation in the Workplace	1.0

What About Credit for Your Cross-Over Skills

You may have a background of training through approved course work and job experience that makes you a candidate to receive college credits in *liberal arts (general education)* courses. These are courses that provide students with a survey of an academic field, such as life or physical science, humanities, arts or social science. For instance, paramedics may request anatomy and physiology courses. Machinists request courses in metallurgy. Police officers and firefighters request courses in ethnic studies, sociology of death and dying, multicultural behavior and non-verbal communication.

These are "cross-over" skills you have developed because your job experiences involve a variety of aspects. Firefighters use physics and math. Managers use business psychology and speech communication.

Ask for these types of general education survey courses only if you have **guided activities** in these areas and have written convincingly about them in your essays.

Copyright ©1980, 1999, 2001 Roslyn Snow

What is a Guided Activity?

A guided activity may be tasks you perform at work that have been evaluated by a manager or result in a work product, a sample of which you can provide as a document.

A guided activity may also be a training session taught by an approved teacher or trainer. It may be recent private instruction by a qualified artist or musician in which you created drawings or paintings or composed or played music. You have samples of the work you produced, or tapes or compact discs of your performance. A guided activity may be participation in a book club or service as a docent in a museum, if it is regular and recent. It may be your own genealogical or historical research if you can produce documents and recorded notes that you used in your research.

A guided activity is not a trip to a museum (even with a docent). It is not foreign travel, even to the great museums and historical sites. It is not private reading or listening to your musical collection. A guided activity must have one of these two elements:

1. It must be an activity that an expert watched you perform and helped you improve.

2. It must be an activity that resulted in a tangible product or document that you can provide for the faculty evaluators to inspect.

Copyright ©1980, 1999, 2001 Roslyn Snow

SAMPLE

REQUEST FOR CREDIT

Transfer to <u>Name of Institution</u>

Course Number	Course Name	Units
Business 100	Intro to Business	3
Business 107	Business Math	3
CIS 100	Intro to Computer Info Svs	3
CIS 134	Excel	3
CIS 191	Local Area Networking	4
English 105	Technical Report Writing	3
Management 100	Applied Management	3
Management 115	Human Relations and Supervision	3
Management 130	Personnel Management	3
Management 210	Applied Communications	3
Marketing 110	Professional Selling	3
Office Management 113	Word Processing Techniques	3
Speech 112	Small Group Processes	3
Speech 114	Developing Leadership	2

> Submit your preliminary **Request for Credit** to your APL Instructor Your Instructor will help you revise it in line with your Educational Plan.

CREATING YOUR EDUCATIONAL PLAN

Your APL Instructor will prepare an educational plan for you so that you are certain all of the course credits you receive through APL will transfer to the accredited college or university of your choice. If you wish to receive an associate's degree or transfer to a four-year college or university that requires specific course prerequisites, this plan will be indispensable.

This Plan will incorporate the courses you have listed on your Request for Credit. It will also serve as a basis for making sure the courses you have chosen on your Request for Credit are appropriate and complete.

Your Instructor will complete this Plan using special forms your college counseling office provides. Your Instructor will have these forms available. Preparing an educational plan is a complicated procedure. Even though you do not have to prepare the plan, you should know what is involved.

Guidelines Your APL Instructor Uses to Prepare Your Educational Plan

---

- ✓ **College Requirements:** If you were starting out as a new student with absolutely no prior learning at the college level, you would need to complete about 60 units to receive your two year associate's degree. This means approximately twenty different courses.

- ✓ **General Education:** Approximately ten to twelve courses must be in "general education" areas: science, art, history, political science, communications and math.

- ✓ **Major Requirements:** Approximately eight courses must be in a major area of study or career area.

- ✓ **Electives:** The remaining two or three courses may be taken from any area of study in the catalog.

Copyright ©1980, 1999, 2001 Roslyn Snow

- Residency: To earn a degree from a college you may need to complete a residency requirement: that is, you may need to complete a minimum number of courses in the classroom at that college. Your APL Instructor will advise you if you need to complete a residency requirement and how it must be met.

- Planning Guide: Every college has different general education, major and elective requirements. Your APL Instructor will use a Planning Guide to be certain that the course credits you earn through APL will transfer to the college or university of your choice.

- You may not meet all course requirements for the school of your choice through your Assessment of Prior Learning. Part of educational planning will be to determine which courses you will need to take at a college, through examination, or through a distance-learning format.

- CLEP: You may meet your general education requirements by passing the College Level Examination Program examinations. Exams are given in English, science, social science, humanities, and math. Your Instructor will help you contact the testing office nearest you and will advise you if the university you wish to attend accepts CLEP.

- Telecourses and Internet Courses: There are both public and private colleges that offer courses broadcast over public or cable television or on video for rental. Most colleges offer classes on the World Wide Web. These courses are accredited and transferable. They range from two to three weeks to a full semester (18 weeks) or quarter (12 weeks). Many have "rolling admission" which means you may enter at any time and receive your credits and grade when you complete all of the assignments or competencies. Your Instructor can give you more details about these courses.

Revising Your Request for Credit

Your preliminary Request for Credit will help both you and your Instructor prepare the final request. You have already listed those classes that represent learning that you described in the essays and documented in the Index.

Your APL Instructor will review your transcripts from schools previously attended to make sure there is no duplication between courses taken and courses requested.

Your certificate, degree, or transfer plan will determine which courses your APL Instructor advises you to keep on your Request for Credit. Trust your Instructor's experience. College transfer information may be very confusing and difficult to interpret.

Your APL Instructor will use the information that follows in guiding you as you prepare your final Request for Credit.

College or University Degree Requirements

There are three different types of college requirements that make up the total academic degree. Courses in these areas are required in differing numbers.

  I.   **General Education Requirements:** These courses cover six areas:

   1. Speech, English writing, logic and reasoning
   2. Physical and natural science
   3. Mathematics
   4. Arts and humanities
   5. Social science and history
   6. Life skills

Colleges select specific courses from their curriculum in each of these categories and require their completion or offer a choice from among a limited number of courses. For instance, most colleges require the completion of a specific course in freshman composition to meet the English writing requirement. A college may select two speech courses from among 10 or 12 that they teach to meet the speech requirement. Another college may offer a choice of four or five speech courses that meet this general education requirement. Still other colleges may offer a choice of a speech course to meet an arts or humanities requirement.

Copyright ©1980, 1999, 2001 Roslyn Snow

II.   Major Requirements: These are courses that represent instruction in a work or professional field: either specific courses or a choice of courses in a single subject as long as the total course credits meet the number required, usually 18 to 24.

If you are transferring to a university, you will complete your Major Requirements at the university.

III.   Electives: A degree is measured in part by the number of course credits you complete. An associate's degree requires 60 units. A bachelor's degree requires 128 to130 course credits. Add up the number of general education requirements and specific major requirements and subtract that number from the total course credits required. The remainder can be filled by *elective* course credits in a transferable area. Some of these elective credits may be in courses in a work-related area, such as business, technology, or management.

The fewer general education and major requirements at the school to which you are transferring, the more elective credits you may use towards your requirements.

Your APL Instructor will know which courses are on the approved list at the college to which you are transferring or from which you are graduating.

Copyright ©1980, 1999, 2001 Roslyn Snow

College or University Degree Planning

ASSOCIATE'S DEGREE

If you want to earn an associate's degree from a college instead of or in addition to a bachelor's degree you need to complete 60 *lower division* course credits covering the three requirements: General Education, Major Requirements and Electives. Most colleges have a residency requirement of 12 to15 college credits that must be taken at the campus in order to graduate even if all other requirements are met. You may be able to use television or Internet classes to count toward your residency requirement, although you are not taking them in a classroom.

You may be required to meet specific requirements in psychology, physical education, and human diversity (sociology, foreign language, multicultural experience).

In some colleges, major requirements can be met only by completing a set of courses in an academic, occupational or technical area. There may be a few options or electives within that set of courses.

In other colleges, major requirements may be met by completing 18 to 24 course credits in a single subject on an approved list, such as business, social science, technology, or communications. There are no specific courses required as long as the required number of course credits is met.

STATE UNIVERSITY

Traditional four-year college and university programs, both public and private, require a great many **general education** courses and some major requirement course prerequisites. These schools prepare recent high school graduates for a professional career. No one knows which discipline the student will enter. He may be a chemist. Therefore, his introductory science courses must be rigorous. He may be an economist; therefore, his mathematics and social science and history training must be rigorous. If he or she becomes a physician, we are all especially grateful that this student will have a thorough background in all general education areas.

You may have a work background that enables you to request some **general education** courses. If you are in the fire services, or you are a police officer, a teacher, or a public service worker, such as social worker or probation worker, you may use your APL course credits to meet a *limited number of* general education requirements at a traditional university.

Your college should have a formal articulation agreement with various universities, spelling out a general education plan that is acceptable for completion of lower division general education requirements. Students meeting this plan receive a certification, which your college Records Office prepares at your APL Instructor's request.

PRIVATE UNIVERSITY TRANSFER

Your APL Instructor has negotiated transfer agreements with several *adult-oriented* universities to which most APL students transfer. These universities offer *external degree programs* designed for working adult students. These may be formal articulation agreements or informal agreements based on precedents. You may earn some **general education** course credits that meet requirements at these universities such as freshman English or speech. Some APL students earn course credits in social science, mathematics, and humanities. Your APL Instructor will help you select the general education courses you are likely to earn. You will need to take **major** requirements at the university in a program designed for working adults. Most of the courses your APL Instructor will approve on your Request for Credit will be useful **elective** credits.

Your Educational Plan

Your APL Instructor has recommended certain colleges or universities that you should attend, schools that allow you to use the maximum number of elective credits from your assessment results. It is wise to trust your APL Instructor to help you make these decisions. Your APL Instructor has prepared an educational plan listing the general education, major and elective courses you are most likely to receive through your APL evaluation and that lead to a degree or transfer to the college or university of your choice. Your Instructor may suggest you delete some courses on your Request for Credit and add others.

Your educational plan will list also the courses you will need *to take* at a college or university in order to meet requirements for admission or to complete a bachelor's degree program.

Copyright ©1980, 1999, 2001 Roslyn Snow

Request for Credit

Use the following checklist to be sure you have followed every step in preparing your Request for Credit.

☐ Have you read each entry in the section of the college catalog titled "Courses" or "Instruction?"

☐ Have you marked courses that relate to your work experience, especially your current experience or the experience that constitutes most of your work career?

☐ Have you marked courses that relate to your life experiences, such as hobbies, volunteer work, public service or private instruction?

☐ Have you eliminated any courses that cover material you are interested in but in which you do not have any guided activities?

☐ Have you eliminated any courses, *even if they are required for a degree or transfer to a university*, in which you do not have documented experiences and for which you have no documents in your Portfolio?

☐ Have you added those courses your APL Instructor has suggested in line with your educational plan.

Send your revised **Request for Credit** to your APL Instructor now.

Copyright ©1980, 1999, 2001 Roslyn Snow

Chapter Five: Petitioning for Credit

You have reviewed your work and life experiences in your Portfolio Essay. You have matched your prior learning to courses that will transfer to the accredited college of your choice to meet your educational goals. You have listed these courses on a Request for Credit.

Now you will develop a **Petition** for each course you are requesting through assessment.

What is a Petition?

A Petition is a one-page summary of the duties and accomplishments you wrote about in your essay and the supporting documents that match one specific course on your Request for Credit.

The faculty evaluators reviewing your Portfolio will have read all of your essays and inspected your documents. They will have looked at the Request for Credit to see what course credits you and your APL Instructor have matched to your prior learning. The **Petition** gives them a one-page worksheet to help them make their decision about whether to grant you the course credits and what grade to apply.

The Petition should include:

1. A copy of the course description taken directly from the college catalog (**Course Description**)
2. The jobs, training and/or life experiences that taught you the knowledge that matches the course description (**Source of Learning**)
3. A summary of the duties and accomplishments you wrote about in your essay that match the course description from the college catalog (**Learning Outcomes**)
4. A list of the documents you have chosen to support your request for each course (**Documents**)

Copyright ©1980, 1999, 2001 Roslyn Snow

Exercise 9: WRITING THE PETITION

Following the sample in this section, write a **Petition** for each course listed on your **Request for Credit**.

Your Petition will highlight what you have covered in your essays. It will be the last part of your Portfolio that the faculty evaluator reads. It should highlight and showcase job duties, accomplishments, projects you worked on, and major responsibilities that relate to each course and are similar to those expected of a student taking the course.

To prepare to write your Petitions, you should re-read your Portfolio Essay, matching tasks and duties, work products and accomplishments to specific courses on your Request for Credit.

Only the faculty evaluators can determine what you learned through your work and life experiences. You can present the basis for their decision in your Petition.

Course Description
Photocopy, cut, and paste the course description from the college catalog at the top of the page. If you have desktop publishing equipment, scan the course descriptions into your text files for each petition.

Source of Learning: List the jobs, training and life experiences that provided the learning you have that is related to this course.

- List the name of the companies or organizations.
- List the positions you held and appropriate dates.
- List the names of training classes.
- List the community organizations.

Learning Outcomes: Highlight the tasks and accomplishments you have written about in your Portfolio Essay that match those expected from students taking this course. Choose tasks and work products from throughout your Portfolio Essay.

- List the activities you did that would be done in this class: "I gave three presentations a week to audiences of more than 100 managers." "I wrote a 20-page report after visiting the manufacturing site."
- Identify the equipment you used and the outcomes: "I created a macro in Excel that ages accounts."

Documentation: Choose the best documents that relate to each petition from your Index to Documents, and list them by number and description

- List documents that illustrate Learning Outcomes.
- Use work sample documents and letters from employers and work colleagues.
- Select and list the most appropriate documents for each separate petition.
- List the documents by document name and number: (Document 101 Letter from J.B. White
Document 148 Sample of Letter I Wrote to Recommend   Purchase of Computer System).

Submit your first three petitions to your APL Instructor now.

SAMPLE PETITION

PETITION

> Office Information Systems 118 ---Advanced Computer Keyboarding (1.5) (9 week course)
>
> **Prerequisite:** Office Information Systems 116
> Provides the opportunity for skill development on the microcomputer. Emphasis on the development of production competency, the ability to make independent decisions, and the responsibility to process high-quality production work commonly found in a variety of situations from many different forms of input. Document processing will include business communications, reports, bound and unbound manuscripts with footnotes, ruled columns, personal datasheets and forms. Language art skills will be reviewed. May be taken for grades or on a credit-no credit basis. Two hours lecture, three hours laboratory. Offered F; S; Sum.

SOURCE OF LEARNING: M. Industries (Global Machine Tool) 1986-91

B.B. Corporation 1991-98

LEARNING OUTCOMES: While employed at M. Industries, I used an IBM DisplayWrite to store and write form letters. I used the DisplayWrite to set up online formats to invoice customers of the four companies operating under M. Industries. At B.B., I produce high-quality management reports and evaluations using an IBM model XT with WordStar or an IBM PS/2 with WORD. I use the word processing features to include management summaries, tables of content, title pages, indexes, and text. Word-processing features that I use include bolding, underlining, and centering text; copying, moving, and deleting text blocks; spell checking and thesaurus features; and column printing. I used WordStar software to write copy for a company newsletter. I used an IBM PC/XT with WordStar software to produce information security documentation, user and desk procedures, business memos, and evaluations. I use mainframe IC/1 graphics software to create charts and graphs included in the reports. I also use TSO, an online mainframe text editor, to create and edit memos and brief documents. Some of the editing features I use in TSO include underlining text, splitting text, page breaks, and copying, moving, and deleting text blocks.

DOCUMENTS:
Document 107, Letter-- J. Gill, Global Machine Tool Corp.
Document 108, Letter-- C. Byrne, B.B. Corp.
Document 109, Draft for "Et Cetera"
Document 114, Information Security Policy
Document 116, Information Security Desk Procedures
Document 120, 121, 122, 123, Sample memos
Document 124, Statement of Direction
Document 125, Project Schedule
Document 126, LAN Security Evaluation Document 160, CQI Team Action Plan

Copyright ©1980, 1999, 2001 Roslyn Snow

Petitions

Use this checklist to be certain you have followed all the steps in creating your Petitions.

☐ Have you cut and pasted the course description from the college catalog for each course at the top of the page? (Suggestion: unless you can scan the course description from the catalog, wait until your petitions have been proofread before doing the final paste-up.)

☐ Have you listed the jobs (company name), training courses and life experiences and dates involved as they are appropriate on the petition under the heading: Source of Learning?

☐ Have you listed the most important job duties, responsibilities, projects, accomplishments and work products as they relate to the subject matter of each course? Have you put this list under the heading: Learning Outcomes?

☐ Have you listed by name and number the most appropriate documents that relate to the duties, responsibilities, projects, accomplishments and products created or services rendered?

Send your APL Instructor all of your petitions for review.

Copyright ©1980, 1999, 2001 Roslyn Snow

Are We There Yet?

All of your writing projects are now over! You have completed a major milestone in writing all of your portfolio essays, selecting appropriate college courses and writing a petition explaining why you are qualified to earn credits in each course.

You will find that the next steps in putting together the Portfolio are simple and straightforward. Continue to pay attention to detail because the format you present will advertise to the faculty evaluators reading your portfolio whether or not you are able to maintain a professional level of excellence in a major project. The evaluators do not know the time you have spent revising your essays. When they see your portfolio it will be as though you have just completed it. They will not see the effort. They will see only the finished look. So do not let down your guard at this point. Keep your eye on the details of the guidelines we are going to give you on assembling all of your portfolio essays and documents.

Copyright ©1980, 1999, 2001 Roslyn Snow

Chapter Six: Assembling the Portfolio

Formatting Guidelines

Margins: 1-inch top, bottom, and right.
                        1.5 inch left to accommodate binding.

Paper: Letter quality computer or reproduction paper.

Spacing: Essays: Double space or 1.5 spaces.
                        Five-space paragraph indentation.
                        Petitions: Single space.
                        Request for Credit: Double space or 1.5 space
                        Index to Documents: Double space or 1.5 spaces.

Page Numbers: Center at top or bottom, left or right: Be consistent.

Headings: Either flush left block or across the page.

XYZ Company
Detroit, Michigan
1985-93
Draftsman or

XYZ Company, Detroit, Michigan, 1985-93, Draftsman

Use **headings** for Education and Training and Life Experiences as necessary.

Copyright ©1980, 1999, 2001 Roslyn Snow

Exercise 10: FRONT MATTER

Front matter consists of **Title Page**, **Permission to Read** and **Contents**.

Contents should be as simple as possible, listing only the key elements in your Portfolio:

- Introduction
- Request for Credit
- Petitions
- Essay
- Index to Documents
- Documents

SAMPLE TITLE PAGE

PORTFOLIO OF PRIOR LEARNING

(Picture of you and business card are attractive here)

YOUR NAME
ADDRESS
CITY STATE ZIP
E-Mail ADDRESS
PHONE NUMBER (DAY TIME NUMBER)
PHONE NUMBER (EVENING)
MONTH YEAR
COLLEGE (college granting the APL units)

Copyright ©1980, 1999, 2001 Roslyn Snow

SAMPLE

PERMISSION TO READ

    I grant permission to _____ College faculty and administration to read and review my Portfolio for the purpose of an assessment of my prior learning.

Signature: _____

Printed Name: _____

Date: _____

SAMPLE TABLE OF CONTENTS

CONTENTS

Introduction	i
Request for Credit	ii
Petitions	iii

Essay
Career Experience 1
    (You may list each job here)
    Education and Training
  (You may list each training course here)
	next number

Life Experience (You may list each hobby, sport or activity)	next number
Index to Documents	iv
Documents	v

Exercise 11: ASSEMBLING THE PORTFOLIO

This is the order in which to put the nine components of your Portfolio:

1. Title Page

2. Permission to Read

3. Table of Contents

4. Introduction

5. Request for Credit

6. Petition

7. Essays (Work, Training, Life Experience in that order)

8. Index to Documents

9. Documents

The sketch on the next page will help you assemble your Portfolio.

Copyright ©1980, 1999, 2001 Roslyn Snow

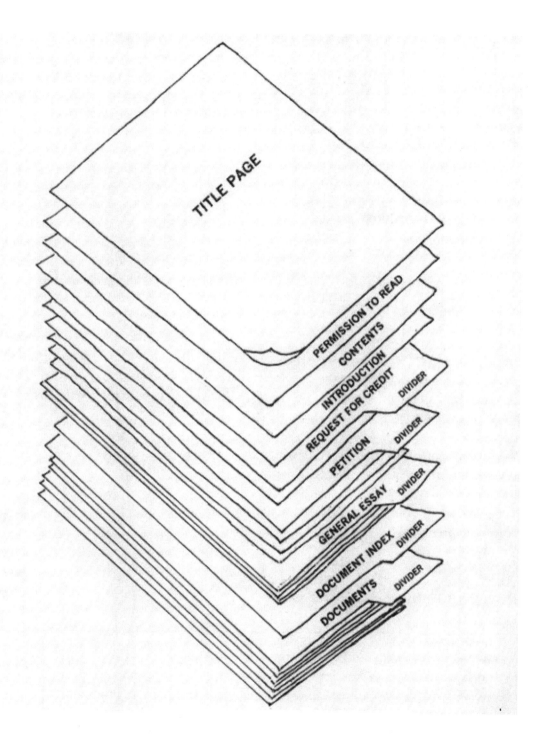

The APL Portfolio

Copyright ©1980, 1999, 2001 Roslyn Snow

How Do I Present My Portfolio?

Bind your Portfolio in sturdy three-ring notebook binders. Use 2.5 inch or 3 inch binders. Use notebook dividers to set apart the last five major sections of your Portfolio:

Request for Credit
Petitions
Essays
Index to Documents
Documents

You may use additional dividers to separate your essays. Use additional dividers to separate every group of 10 documents.

If you have extensive multiple page documents that will not fit in your notebook binder, put one copy only in a separate accordion-fold file and put the document number on the file. Do this only when the document represents a sample of your original graphics or production work and an excerpt will not be sufficient. *Otherwise you should include only a small excerpt of pages from a multiple page document.*

Put blueprints and large drawings in a tube or other container and place the document number label on the container.

Note on your Index to Documents the location of any documents not in your notebook binder.

How Do I Submit My Portfolio?

Send *one* copy of your Portfolio to your Instructor for proofreading and review before you make copies. Send your Portfolio by private carrier, such as UPS, FedEx or US Post Office certified mail. This is a very important document and may contain some original papers. Protect it from loss.

Assembling the Portfolio

You have reached the *final step*: Assembling the entire Portfolio. Your APL Instructor will proofread your Portfolio only if it has been correctly formatted. If not, it will be returned to you for corrections.

Formatting the Essays

If you cannot meet all of these suggestions because of your computer equipment, please do the best you can. Your goal is to present a readable, neat format so that the faculty evaluators can find each component of your Portfolio easily.

- Use double or 1.5 lines spacing for all essays.

- Use single spacing for petitions.

- Use a five-space paragraph indentation in all of your essays.

- Leave ample margins to create a neat appearance, especially on the left side of the page to accommodate the three-hole punch.

Copyright ©1980, 1999, 2001 Roslyn Snow

- Aid the reader by using headings for each job change, education and training and life experience.

- Number the essays consecutively starting with your first job essay and ending with your last life experience. (If your job essays end on page 50, your first training essay page will be 51.)

- Center page numbers at the top or bottom of the page so your document label does not cover them.

- Front Matter pages include title page, permission to read, and table of contents. These need not be numbered.

- Place labeled notebook dividers to separate these sections of your Portfolio:

    - Request for Credit
    - Petitions
    - Essays
    - Index to Documents
    - Documents

- Place labeled notebook dividers to separate every 10 documents.

You must be sure that:

- Each document label contains both the document number and a caption with a name or descriptor: "These are excerpts from a 40 page briefing I wrote and delivered at the Quality Control Meeting."

- Each label is placed on the upper right hand corner of the document's first page-- even if it conceals some of the document. The labels need to be clearly visible.

- Request for Credit and Petitions match. There should be a petition for each course on the Request for Credit.

Copyright ©1980, 1999, 2001 Roslyn Snow

- All essays are numbered consecutively starting with the first job essay and ending with the last life experience essay.

- Your Portfolio must be in a three-ring notebook binder and completely formatted before it is proofread.

Re-Send your Portfolio by certified mail, FedEx, or UPS to your Instructor before making any copies. Your Instructor will return your Portfolio with corrections marked and suggestions for revision

Proofreading the Portfolio

Your APL Instructor will now read your Portfolio all the way through for the first time.

By this time the basic structure of your essays should be correct and you should have sufficient wealth of detail. However, if there are problems in these areas, your Instructor will let you know where and how to revise.

Your Instructor will look at your petitions in relation to your essays and documents and your educational plan to help you get good results in the assessment of your prior learning.

Your Instructor will check for errors in spelling, punctuation and grammatical structure, as well as the inevitable typographical errors that occur in a large written project.

You are responsible for presenting an error-free final copy. Your APL Instructor may not present your portfolio for evaluation until it is in correct format and free of typographical and mechanical errors. Take the time now to make every correction shown and every revision suggested before final submission.

If your Portfolio requires extensive revision and re-writing, your APL Instructor may require you to re-submit one copy for additional proofreading before final submission.

Assessment of Prior Learning
Proofreading Instructions

To _____:
From: _____, APL Instructor
Date:_____

    I have proofread your Portfolio, and it is ready for corrections before submitting to the college for evaluation. I have marked corrections in your Portfolio and circled areas below that require you to make changes or revisions.

1. I have marked your errors in spelling, punctuation and grammar and suggested corrections for you to make. *Make each correction shown.* If you have errors, you may not receive credits for your work.

2. Check that your essay pages are numbered consecutively, starting with your first job essay and ending with your last life experience.

3. Check that all essay pages are spaced double or 1.5 spaces.
   - Headings should be single-spaced.
   - Petitions should be single-spaced.
   - Request for Credit and Index to Documents should be double-spaced.

4. Eliminate unnecessary headers and footers.

5. Check that you have a Petition for each class listed on your Request for Credit.

6. Check that each document is labeled correctly and the correct number is listed on the document signal in your essay.

7. Check that each document is listed correctly on your Index to Documents and Petitions.

8. Be certain each work sample document is labeled, using a name or descriptor to explain what the documents is and what you did to produce it.

9. Make sure you have pasted or scanned the course description from the college catalog on your Petition.

Copyright ©1980, 1999, 2001 Roslyn Snow

10. Use notebook dividers to separate: Request for Credit, Petitions, Essays, Index to Document, Documents and every ten Documents.

11. Bind your Portfolio in a three-ring notebook binder of enough depth to close completely.

Send **three** copies of your Portfolio to your APL Instructor by Certified Mail, FedEx, UPS or another reliable delivery company. Your APL Instructor will let you know if more copies are required. Keep your original and all original documents.

Copyright ©1980, 1999, 2001 Roslyn Snow

Chapter Seven: Assessment

Exercise 12: REVISION AND FINAL SUBMISSION

Once your APL Instructor has approved your corrections and accepted your final submission, your assessment can be scheduled.

Your APL Instructor or program administrator will contact you to complete all requirements for the assessment to begin. These include current registration at the college granting the credits and payment of all tuition and assessment fees.

Faculty evaluators who have taught the courses you have requested will be chosen to evaluate your Portfolio.

Faculty can grant college credits and, in many programs, can assign a letter grade in each of the courses they approve on your Request for Credit. These may be A, B, C, D, or Cr (Credit) grades, depending on the regulations in the college catalog.

How and When Will I Get My Results?

Your Portfolio will be assessed within three or four weeks. A faculty evaluator may contact you during this time to ask you questions or discuss what you wrote in your essays. Usually the evaluators will have enough information from your Portfolio and they will not contact you.

What Happens After My Assessment?

Your APL Instructor will let you know your results immediately.

Copyright ©1980, 1999, 2001 Roslyn Snow

The college that grants your APL units is governed by regulations affecting how many Assessment of Prior Learning credits it can allow you to receive. Its regional accrediting association sets these regulations. The faculty evaluators may have granted more course credits than allowed. Your APL Instructor will help you decide which courses credits to record on your college transcript.

The faculty evaluators may have rejected some of the courses you requested. Your APL Instructor will be able to tell you why. You may have an opportunity to re-petition for courses that were not granted if the faculty evaluators are willing to review additional information and documents.

After assessment, the courses approved will be posted to your college transcript. Your official transcript will be mailed to the college or university of your choice at your request. The college granting your APL units is the "sending institution." The college or university to which you are transferring is the "receiving institution." In some cases you may be continuing toward your degree at the same college that is awarding your APL units. In that case, your APL units will be added to your official transcript at that school.

Your APL Instructor will review your educational plan to see which courses you need to take to complete your degree. Some of these courses may be taken over the Internet or through video broadcast. Others must be taken at the campus of the college or university you are or will be attending. Stay in touch with your APL Instructor until you have received your degree or have been referred to a college or university counselor who will take you the rest of the way to your goal.

Copyright ©1980, 1999, 2001 Roslyn Snow

Congratulations.

You have reached an important milestone toward your educational and career goals. We are glad to have been able to guide your way, and we look forward to hearing from you when you reach the next steps on your path whether they are advanced degrees or career promotion. We know your future holds both.

Copyright ©1980, 1999, 2001 Roslyn Snow

CPSIA information can be obtained at www.ICGtesting.com
Printed in the USA
240831LV00011B/23/P